America
Comes of Age

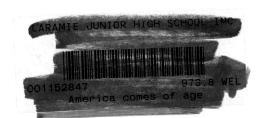

THE MAKING OF AMERICA

America Comes of Age

Donna Wells

RAINTREE
STECK-VAUGHN
PUBLISHERS

A Harcourt Company

Austin · New York
www.steck-vaughn.com

Published by Raintree Steck-Vaughn Publishers, an imprint of Steck-Vaughn Company

Developed by Discovery Books
Editor: Sabrina Crewe
Designer: Sabine Beaupré
Maps and charts: Stefan Chabluk

Raintree Steck-Vaughn Publishers Staff
Publishing Director: Walter Kossmann
Art Director: Max Brinkmann
Editor: Shirley Shalit

Library of Congress Cataloging-in-Publication Data
Wells, Donna Koren, 1951-
    America comes of age / Donna Wells.
        p. cm. -- (Making of America)
    Includes bibliographical references and index.
    ISBN 0-8172-5708-X
    1. United States--History--1856-1898--Juvenile literature. [1. United
States--History--1865-1898.] I. Title. II. Making of America (Austin, Tex.)
    E661.W45 2000
    973.8--dc21

                                                    00-031078

Printed and bound in the United States of America
1 2 3 4 5 6 7 8 9 0 IP 04 03 02 01 00

Acknowledgments
Cover Corbis; pp. 7, 8, 9, 10, 11, 12 Corbis; p. 13 The Granger Collection; pp. 17, 18, 20, 22 Corbis; p. 23 The Granger Collection; p. 26 Corbis; p. 29 The Granger Collection; pp. 30, 31, 33, 34, 35, 36, 40 Corbis; p. 41 The Granger Collection; pp. 42, 45 Corbis; p. 46 The Granger Collection; pp. 48, 49 Corbis; pp. 51, 54 The Granger Collection; pp. 56, 57 Corbis; p. 59 The Granger Collection; pp. 64, 65, 68, 69, 70 Corbis; p. 71 The Granger Collection; p. 72 Corbis; p. 76 The Granger Collection; pp. 78, 79 Corbis; p. 80 The Granger Collection; pp. 81, 82, 83, 85, 86 Corbis.

Cover illustration: This painting from the late 1800s shows immigrants arriving in New York Harbor on a steamship from Europe.

Contents

Introduction

If the Civil War marked the end of the slavery era in American history, then the Reconstruction period that followed set the stage for the vast changes that would soon take place in the nation. Everyone knew that the country faced a long period of uncertainty, rebuilding, and mending. One purpose of Reconstruction, which began in 1865 and ended in 1877, was to bring the Southern states back into the Union. Another was to achieve equality for former slaves and recognition of their rights as equal citizens under the law.

Congress passed new laws, including the Civil Rights Act of 1866, guaranteeing blacks citizenship, the right to work, and the right to own property. For a short time, black people used the protections established by law to make significant social and political gains. However, as white Southerners regained control of national and local government, African Americans found their liberties being taken away once more.

The devastation created by the Civil War, which ended in 1865, had caused setbacks for many. The economy of the South was nearly ruined. Farms and cities, machinery and crops—much had been destroyed. And now there was no more slavery, the system of unpaid labor on which Southern prosperity had depended.

However, in the country as a whole and particularly in the North, there were huge opportunities for those willing to venture into manufacturing industries. Between 1865 and 1873, the country's manufacturers increased their output by 75 percent. During the same period, 3 million immigrants entered the United States, providing workers for the many new factories. For the first time, there were more industrial workers than there were farmers. The United States had entered the Industrial Age.

1

The Age of Progress

M any developments in science and technology were behind the new industries that developed in the Industrial Age of the late 1800s. These inventions changed not only industry, but the daily lives of millions of people in America.

The Centennial Exhibition

In 1876, the United States celebrated the 100th anniversary, or centennial, of the Declaration of Independence. Part of this celebration was a huge exhibition in Philadelphia, called the "Centennial International Exhibition." It opened on May 10, 1876, with the purpose of highlighting advances in science and technology.

Several exhibition halls were specially built for the occasion on a site covering more than 450 acres in the city's Fairmount Park. Each state had its own building to showcase its exhibits. The states focused on the miracles of modern machinery, and more than 50 foreign nations also exhibited their latest art and inventions. Displayed in the Manufacturing Hall were department

The theme of the 1876 Centennial Exhibition in Philadelphia was "Progress of the Age." It celebrated the huge industrial and scientific developments that had taken place in the mid-1800s.

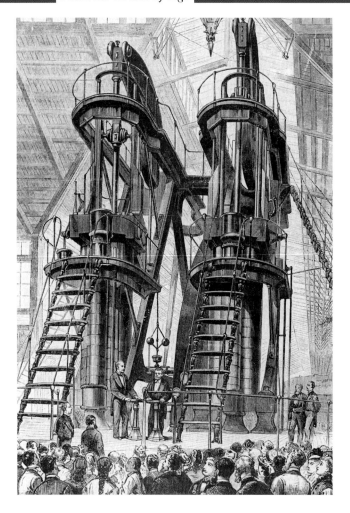

President Ulysses S. Grant opens the exhibit of the Corliss steam engine at the Philadelphia Centennial Exhibition. The engine was over 40 feet (12 m) tall and had a horsepower of 1,400. Although other engines of the time offered similar power, none was so impressive to look at.

stores filled with many different goods. The Horticultural Hall held landscaped gardens in greenhouses; and galleries exhibited paintings and sculptures.

The Machinery Hall housed the newest inventions. Two months after he made the first telephone call in Boston, Alexander Graham Bell demonstrated his discovery in Philadelphia. Many people also saw typewriters for the first time. Recently developed refrigerators and a new kind of printing press were on display, and so was the bicycle. The most amazing exhibit was the new Corliss steam engine, the largest ever created.

Some criticized the exhibition because it was not representative of the entire country. None of the exhibits addressed the needs of black or Native American people. There was a Woman's Pavilion where "women's industrial talents" were displayed, but only in a superficial way. Feminists of the day, including Susan B. Anthony and Elizabeth Cady Stanton, staged a protest against the exhibition on July 4, 1876, and released their own "Woman's Declaration of Independence."

Yet, in many ways, the Philadelphia Centennial Exhibition represented a turning point, a symbolic beginning of the Industrial Age in America. Almost 10 million people, over 20 percent of the country's population, attended the exhibition to see new American inventions for themselves. The number of people who came was extraordinary, since most worked six days a week and had to come a long way.

The Great Inventors

The wondrous machines on display in Philadelphia reflected the work of many inventors of the period. From the time he was a teenager, Alexander Graham Bell had been working to develop a way to transmit speech electrically. In 1874, he had discovered that a steady electrical current could be used to transmit human sounds. By 1876, he had obtained a patent for the electric telephone. Telephone lines were laid between New York and Chicago. For the first time, long distance calls could be made between two of the largest cities in the country. The first central telephone operation was created in Connecticut. At first, only 21 people were connected to it. By the turn of the century, 1.3 million telephones were in service.

Soon after Bell's invention, the Western Union Telegraph Company asked inventor Thomas Alva Edison to focus on developing a less expensive form of telephone technology. Instead, Edison looked for a way to record a voice which could then be played through a speaker. For his new machine, he attached a telephone to a needle that etched grooves onto a cylinder in response to sounds. When the cylinder was rotated by a hand crank, the sounds played back and the phonograph was born. Edison had invented the phonograph to be used as a dictating machine, but it quickly became more popular as a record player. Music could be recorded onto records which were then placed on a turntable and played using a needle.

Edison was also working to produce an electric light bulb. He demonstrated his new bulb in 1879, using a filament of carbonized cotton thread that had been developed by African American Latimer Lewis. The invention would eventually allow entire cities to be lit by electricity rather than by gaslights. This happened first in 1892, when the Pearl Street central power station in New York City was completed. By 1900, 20 million electric lamps had been produced.

On November 29, 1877, Edison sang "Mary Had a Little Lamb" into his phonograph, and the machine played his voice back to him. It was the first time that sound had been successfully recorded and replayed. The phonograph soon became popular for playing recorded music.

"Genius is 1 percent inspiration and 99 percent perspiration."

Thomas Edison

Thomas Alva Edison (1847–1931)

Thomas Edison was born in Milan, Ohio. By the time he was ten years old, he had built a chemistry laboratory in his home. When he was still quite young, he lost most of his hearing in an accident. In spite of this handicap, Edison began his own business, selling newspapers on trains. That job allowed him to spend time around the telegraphers who worked on the railroads, and he quickly became fascinated with telegraphy. Edison was later hired as a telegrapher himself, and began experimenting with electricity.

Thomas Edison in 1925, holding the first successful light bulb that he had produced in 1879.

Edison tested thousands of materials before he finally developed the electric light bulb, which he successfully demonstrated in 1879. Two years later, he built the first electric power plant in Manhattan, New York.

In his lifetime, Edison obtained over a thousand patents for inventions ranging from the light bulb to the stock ticker, a machine that printed out prices of company stocks. He also patented the mimeograph, which made duplicate copies of documents by pressing ink through a stencil. Edison became known as the "Wizard of Menlo Park," after the town in New Jersey where he lived and built his laboratory.

Mass Production

While some people developed exciting new inventions, others took existing machines and produced them in large numbers for the growing American market. Albert A. Pope had seen the bicycle at the 1876 Philadelphia Centennial Exhibition. Bicycles had been in limited use for many years, but Pope realized they could become a popular mode of transportation. In 1878, he converted his sewing-machine factory into a bicycle manufacturing plant and was soon producing thousands of bicycles a year. Each one sold for approximately $100.

Lewis E. Waterman revolutionized writing when he found a way to improve on the messy, time-consuming method of constantly dipping a pen in an inkwell. In 1884, he produced the first "fountain pen," which held ink inside the pen. Soon, they were being made in thousands. A few years later, pencils began to be mass produced, selling at two for a penny. And writing paper could now be manufactured, making it affordable to almost everyone.

This industrialization transformed the economy of the nation. When the Civil War began, only about $1 billion was invested in manufacturing in America. By the turn of the century, nearly $10 billion was invested. In 1860, the nation's wealth was estimated to be about $16 billion and agriculture was still the dominant force in the economy. By 1890, the national wealth had grown to $65 billion; and by 1900, the value of manufactured products was double that of agricultural goods.

New Kinds of Transportation

Transportation methods also changed in the late 1800s as electricity and new machinery opened up opportunities for inventors. In rural areas, people continued to rely on horses and wagons to get around. But in the cities, with their large populations and crowded streets, there was a need for public transportation. In 1873, William Smith Hallidie introduced the cable car in San Francisco. By 1882, there were nearly 20,000 cable cars operating in cities like San Francisco, Denver, and Los Angeles.

Cable cars, however, were expensive to build and maintain. The first electric streetcar, invented by Stephen Dudley Field, was tried in New York City in 1874. Frank

By the 1890s, due to mass production, bicycles had become available to many. Bicycle-riding enjoyed a boom, and not only men but women rode them by the hundreds. One result of the craze was that women began to wear shorter skirts for the first time.

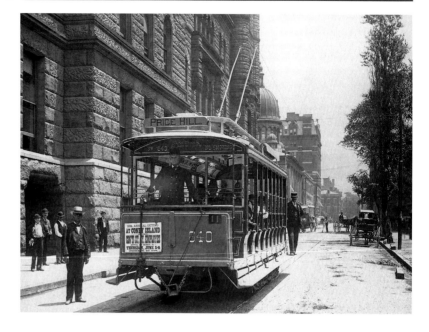

By the turn of the century, 30,000 electric streetcars were operating in cities across the country. As cities grew, the cars provided an efficient transportation network for the booming population. The networks spread outward to bring commuters to work from the new communities that were developing on city outskirts.

Sprague, an engineer from Virginia, later improved the design of streetcars, leading to wider use. By 1888, Sprague's hometown of Richmond had an entire streetcar system. Within two years, 200 other cities had built similar networks.

Trains Unite the Nation

The development and expansion of the railroads brought about some of the biggest changes to the United States in the late 1800s. As factories produced more and more goods, the railroads were there to move these goods from one place to another. The railroads began to unite the country as nothing else had before. By 1890, there were four rail routes from the east coast to the west coast. Chicago, the central hub of the rail lines, had trains arriving and departing at the rate of 15 per hour. By 1900, railroads were the country's largest industry and largest employer.

Railroads helped industrial growth and changed the daily lives of Americans as goods became more accessible. Farmers had a quicker means to transport their products. Coal and other resources could be distributed more easily. Increasingly, freight was carried by rail rather than along roads or canals.

"An almost total revolution has taken place, and is yet in progress, in every branch and in every relation of the world's industrial and commercial system."

Economist David Wells, 1899

Soon, cities and towns sprang up along the rail lines as more and more people and goods moved around the country. Telephone and telegraph lines quickly followed, strung alongside the railroads.

Trains were even responsible for regulating time. Until the 1800s, the United States did not have standard time zones. People usually set their clocks by their towns' main clocks, which were in turn set by the sun at noon, and so the time varied by minutes across the nation. But the arrival of coast-to-coast rail travel required the establishment of set times so that people would know when trains arrived or departed. In 1883, the United States Department of Transportation created standard time zones across the country.

As Chicago became the center of the railroad industry, the Illinois Central Railroad was one of many that helped open up the United States to travelers and gave businesses a safe and speedy way to move their products around the country. This 1882 poster was an advertisement for the company.

The Impact of New Inventions

Each new product generated the need for a workforce. Sometimes, just a few workers were needed. At other times, entire industries would spring up around an invention, such as the railroad sleeping car.

It is said that necessity is the mother of invention, meaning that things get invented when there is a need for them. This was true in the United States of the nineteenth century, as Americans spread out across their nation. The telephone was invented because of the need to communicate more effectively across distances. Barbed wire was invented because ranchers in the West needed a cheaper means of fencing in their land and livestock. The telegraph, telephone, electric light bulb, and streetcar all spread from one city to the next. As transportation and communication lines increased, the inventions of the Industrial Age changed not only the economy, but the way people lived.

"There is in all the past nothing to compare with the rapid changes now going on in the civilized world. . . . The snail's pace . . . has suddenly become the headlong rush of the locomotive, speeding faster and faster."

Henry George, Social Problems, *1883*

The Industrial Age and Beyond

In 1878, the United States was rushing into a period of economic expansion based on industrial production that would last for 20 years. The Industrial Age brought about huge economic changes. In 1879, the value of all manufactured goods was about $5.4 billion. By the turn of the century, that value had increased to $13 billion. Iron and steel production drove much of the expansion. In 1880, about 1.4 million tons (1.27 million metric tons) of steel were produced. By 1900, approximately 11 million tons (9.98 million metric tons) were being produced annually.

During the twentieth century, a second industrial revolution occurred. The first revolution had relied on steel, iron ore, gold, and silver. The new revolution focused on lighter metals and synthetic products such as plastic and man-made fibers.

Today, there is growing evidence that we are in the middle of a third industrial revolution based not just on products, but on information and services. The emergence of the computer and, more recently, the Internet, is increasingly driving the economy.

2

The Gilded Age

T he late 1800s were a time of great economic expansion and huge riches for some. But the costs of this growth were paid by poorer people in society. Depression, social problems, unemployment, and corruption bubbled beneath the wealthy surface of American life.

The Panic of 1873

The rapid growth of the railroad industry after the Civil War helped fuel the industrial boom that began in the Northeast and spread quickly across the country. By 1890, all the major cities in the country were connected by rail lines. However, it was the same railroad industry that brought the growing economy to a sudden halt in 1873.

Jay Cooke, an agent for the United States Treasury, had sold $3 billion in government bonds to help pay for the cost of the Civil War. Because he earned a commission on each bond he sold, Cooke was a very wealthy man. He then started to sell bonds for the Northern Pacific Railroad to pay for the building of a second railroad line across the country. Unfortunately, even Cooke's powerful banking firm could not sell enough bonds to raise the necessary $100 million. The firm used nearly all its cash reserves to try to save the project, but it could not find enough buyers, and Cooke's friends in Congress refused to help him. In September 1873, Jay Cooke and Company was forced to close. When word of the financial problem spread, panic set in, and 37 other banks and financial institutions linked to the bonds also collapsed. Three days after the Panic of 1873 began, the

New York Stock Exchange stopped all trading because of the fear that the entire U.S. economy would collapse. People rushed to cash in their bonds. When the Northern Pacific Railroad failed, several other companies that were being financed with bonds failed also.

The Depression

The entire country soon fell into a depression, a period when a nation's economic activity slows down and many people become unemployed. Workers were laid off not just by the railroads, but by the banks that financed the railroads and the industries that supported them, such as the steel industry. Within three years, half of the country's railroad companies and steel companies had gone out of business.

Even those who were not involved with the railroads fell on hard times. Demand for goods dropped, causing production to fall. Factories were forced to lay off workers, increasing economic problems. By the end of 1873, over 5,000 large companies were out of business. As unemployment grew, the services of doctors, lawyers, and other professionals were not used as often, and most had to cut their fees. Many immigrants who could no longer find work returned to their native countries. The economic disaster even spilled over into farming as the price of everything, including land, dropped.

The Rise of the Robber Barons

A group of clever businessmen used the depression to purchase failing companies and expand their own interests into vast monopolies. Inventors and great industrialists were linked as the Industrial Age progressed. Yet, while inventors were viewed in a positive light, the industrialists came to be known as the "robber barons." These robber barons saw that the new oil and steel industries could be developed into the backbone of the American Industrial Age. This group of ambitious, often ruthless businessmen was willing to exploit the American workforce in order to increase their own wealth and power.

Steel is made from iron, and large reserves of iron ore had been discovered in the Midwest, making iron both plentiful and more affordable. In addition to this, an Englishman, Henry Bessemer, perfected a new way of producing steel. A similar method had already been tried by William Kelly from Kentucky, but when the Bessemer process was brought to the United States in 1864, it revolutionized steel production. The man who saw and acted on its potential was Andrew Carnegie.

By 1873, Carnegie acquired control of the first major steel company that used the Bessemer process. Because steel was needed even during the depression that followed the Panic of 1873, Carnegie continued to expand his business. He cut his prices in order to win business from other steel producers. He also bargained for lower transportation rates with the railroads, again undercutting his competition. Eventually he bought out, or forced out, much of his competition.

Standard Oil

At the same time as the iron and steel industry was growing, oil was also changing the face of industrial America. In 1859, a well had been drilled in Pennsylvania, providing a reliable source of oil. In 1860, half a million barrels of oil were produced. The demand for oil was so great that soon western Pennsylvania was dotted with oil wells.

Oil taken out of the ground has to be refined, or purified, before it is used, and so refineries were built to meet this demand. In 1863, John D. Rockefeller and his partners built an oil refinery in Ohio. This was the beginning of what would become the huge Standard Oil Company. Rockefeller bought out his competitors, the other refineries, whenever he could. He also arranged cheap transportation costs with the railroads so he could cut prices. This helped him gain control of the oil industry. In the early years of the oil boom, there were over 1,000 oil producers and refiners. But by 1900, when 60 million

The Bessemer process, seen here, was developed in the 1860s to make steel from iron and other elements. The steel industry went on to transform transportation and building in the United States. Two of the leading "robber barons," Andrew Carnegie and John Pierpont Morgan, were industrialists who started in the railroads but then made fortunes in the steel industry.

"The man of wealth [should] consider all surplus revenues which come to him simply as trust funds, which he is called upon to administer."

Andrew Carnegie, 1889

17

was As the depression raged in the 1870s, Cornelius Vanderbilt, who made a fortune in shipping before the Civil War, was expanding his railroad empire. By the time he died in 1877, he was worth $100 million.

"I know of nothing more despicable and pathetic than a man who devotes all the waking hours of the day to making money for money's sake. What people seek most cannot be bought with money."

John D. Rockefeller, 1909

barrels of oil were being pumped annually, 85 percent of the industry was controlled by Rockefeller. He did not try to buy the wells, but instead gained control of the refining and transportation industries needed to bring the oil to market. It appeared that Standard Oil would do anything, even use illegal business practices, in order to keep control of the oil industry.

The Power of the Industrialists

Perhaps no one represented the robber barons better than John Pierpont Morgan. Like the other industrialists, he was accused of choking competition for his own personal gain. On the base of his banking business, Morgan built a financial empire in the railroad industry and gained control over half of the rail lines in the country. Other businesses invested their money in Morgan's empire. Using the vast cash resources provided by his investors, Morgan then was able to establish the United States Steel Company.

The robber barons were successful because they were able to squash their competition, and because they understood the power of the Industrial Age and the opportunities it offered. They also knew that continued economic growth required constant adjustments. Each of them was willing to make frequent changes in production schedules, in equipment and machinery, and in their workforces. The industrialists were also responsible for a basic change in the American economy. No longer would the country rely on small industries to fuel its growth. Powerful companies had much greater control over the market.

The robber barons usually sought to dominate an entire industry, from the raw materials, such as iron ore, to the development and delivery of the product, such as steel supports. This kind of control is known as a monopoly. Once they had established a monopoly, the robber barons were able to set higher prices for their goods. They could also determine what could be shipped where and when. The robber barons ran industries that every community relied on.

The Robber Barons

John Pierpont Morgan (1837–1913) followed in his father's footsteps and became a banker. Eventually, he formed his own banking firm, J.P. Morgan & Company, and expanded it until he became one of the most powerful financial figures in the country. At the same time, he gained control of several local railroads and merged them into larger, regional organizations. Then he turned his attention to the steel industry, forming the U.S. Steel Company. In its time, it was the world's largest corporation.

Andrew Carnegie (1835–1919) was born in Scotland. He emigrated to the United States in 1848, where he began working in a textile mill. Although he had no formal education, Carnegie learned from each of his experiences. In time, he began working for the Pennsylvania Railroad as a telegrapher. He worked hard, was continually promoted, and began to invest in oil exploration and railroads. Carnegie later sold his interests in other industries and concentrated on iron and steel. As he said, "Put all your eggs in one basket, and then watch that basket." By the turn of the century, Carnegie controlled one-quarter of all the iron and steel produced in America.

James Jerome Hill (1838–1916) was a Canadian who also made his fortune in the railroads. In 1878, he and his partners bought out the St. Paul and Pacific Railroad. By purchasing several smaller lines, he built a line that ran from the Canadian border north of St. Paul, Minnesota, westward to Seattle, Washington. Hill then pulled all his holdings into one company, the Great Northern Railway Company. His ruthless control of railroads, and banking and finance interests, were criticized by many who called him the "Empire Builder."

John D. Rockefeller (1838–1919) was born to a working-class family in New York and grew up in Cleveland, Ohio. In 1863, along with a group of investors, Rockefeller built his first oil refinery. Eventually, Rockefeller formed the Standard Oil Company, which took over the refinery business in 1870. Just eight years later, the Rockefeller family had expanded its business to control most of the oil refineries and the oil transportation operations in the country. Eventually, Standard Oil was declared a monopoly and was forced to dissolve, by which time Rockefeller was worth nearly $1 billion. Although he was viewed as a ruthless villain by many Americans, Rockefeller gave nearly half of his personal fortune to charity.

Cities needed steel to construct bridges and buildings, and railroads carried the nation's passengers and freight. Banks and insurance companies were dependent on large industries to make money, and workers were forced to accept poor employment conditions.

The Sherman Antitrust Act

The situation provoked comment in the press. In 1881, journalist and lawyer Henry Demarest Lloyd wrote about the Standard Oil monopoly in the publication *Atlantic Monthly*. A few years later, the labor leader Eugene V. Debs exposed problems in the mining industry in *Arena* magazine. In response to growing public dissatisfaction, the federal government decided to step in.

Free trade, in which everybody has an opportunity to compete in buying and selling a product, was restrained by the monopolies of the rich industrialists. In the United

This cartoon from 1897 shows a trusting Uncle Sam, who represents the United States. He is being robbed by two prosperous figures representing the rich industrialists who had come to dominate the American economy.

States at the time, there were no federal laws that prohibited a company from establishing a monopoly in a particular business. In 1890, however, Congress passed the Sherman Antitrust Act which made it illegal for companies to join together to stop competition. The Act included companies that operated in more than one state as well as those that traded with foreign nations. The purpose of the Act was to increase competition and therefore hold down prices for the consumer. Unfortunately, the Act was poorly worded and hastily passed by Congress. Critics charged that legislators were more concerned with quieting down the public protest about monopolies than they were with really improving the economic situation caused by them.

The first test came in 1895, during the presidency of Grover Cleveland. The American Sugar Company was brought to court and charged under the Sherman Antitrust Act. The Supreme Court found in favor of the company, noting that it hadn't actually restricted trade, or buying and selling, even though it controlled 98 percent of the sugar refining industry. The Supreme Court decision showed that the Act was almost totally useless. If the American Sugar Company wasn't found guilty, then nor would any other company be guilty under the Act. This proved to be true. The large corporations, with the robber barons as their leaders, continued to monopolize entire industries for several years.

The Election of 1896

By 1896, Americans had become dissatisfied with President Cleveland's administration, which appeared to support the robber barons. The presidential election of 1896 reflected the growing conflict between big business and the working man, between the industrialists in the East and farmers in the South and West.

Out of the conflict and confusion of the time emerged William Jennings Bryan, a former congressman from Nebraska. In 1896, the Democratic party chose Bryan instead of Cleveland as its candidate. The People's party, or Populists, which was organized in 1892, also backed Bryan as its candidate.

Bryan contrasted sharply with the Republican candidate, William McKinley. The election campaign highlighted one way of life against another. During the course of the election, Bryan traveled the country and made hundreds of speeches, arguing that agriculture, not industry, was the basis for the country's economy. He opposed the power of the robber barons and supported working people. Yet, in the end, it was McKinley who won the election, reflecting the growing understanding that industry was the future of the country. Americans hoped that he would be able to accomplish what Cleveland had not: reining in the monopolies.

William Jennings Bryan (1860–1925)

Bryan was born in Illinois to Silas and Mariah Bryan. His father was a lawyer, state senator, and circuit court judge. Bryan went to college in Illinois to study law, and then moved to Nebraska. He was twice elected to Congress, in 1890 and 1892, where he campaigned for policies to help farmers.

After he failed to be reelected in 1894, Bryan became editor of the Omaha *World Herald* newspaper, but continued to speak in public on behalf

Williams Jennings Bryan in 1898.

of working people. He became the champion of the free silver movement and won many votes as the Democratic party's presidential candidate in 1896. He lost the election, however, and went on to be defeated twice more in the presidential elections of 1900 and 1908.

From 1901 to 1913, Bryan edited the *Commoner*, a newspaper for working people. In 1912, he became secretary of state under President Woodrow Wilson, but resigned in 1915 in protest at the United States' growing involvement in World War I.

Later in life, Bryan, a fundamental Christian, transferred his spirited campaigning from politics to religion. He believed that only the Bible's story of creation should be taught in schools, and that Darwin's theory of evolution should be banned. In 1925, he took part in the famous Scopes Trial, prosecuting a Tennessee teacher, John Scopes, who violated a state law by teaching evolution in his classroom. Bryan won the trial, and died a week later.

The Gold-Silver Debate

Another issue central to the 1896 election, and Bryan's campaign, was the nation's money. At the time, the United States used gold as the basis of its finances. This meant that the money printed by the government, and used by everybody, represented gold held by the Treasury. The gold "backed" the money in circulation and gave it its value. Bankers and rich industrialists backed the gold standard because it kept the value of their money at a high level.

A debate had raged across the nation for several years between those who favored keeping the gold standard and those who thought silver should be used instead. The Populists and other "Silverites" believed the United States government should establish a value for silver, and then buy all silver mined and turn it into coins. This would increase the amount of money in circulation and so it would decrease the value of the dollar. Such a plan would benefit poorer people. The country's farmers were in debt, and the lower value of the dollar would help them in two ways. It would reduce the amount of their debts and it would cause the price of farm products to rise. A cheaper, silver-backed dollar would also cause wages to rise for workers, and it would benefit the silver mining communities of the West. In addition, increasing the amount of available money would force banks to be more competitive and to offer lower interest rates on loans.

While Bryan campaigned for free silver in 1896, McKinley's Republican platform was based on keeping the gold standard. When McKinley won the election, the gold standard was assured. In 1900, Congress passed the Currency, or Gold Standard, Act, which said that gold would continue to be the basis of U.S. currency.

"You shall not press down upon the brow of labor this crown of thorns, you shall not crucify mankind upon a cross of gold."

William Jennings Bryan, July 8, 1896

This 1895 cartoon shows President Cleveland trying to defend his financial policy against free silver supporters in Congress. The president believed in keeping gold as the standard unit of value in the United States.

The "Gilded Age"

The increasing concentration of wealth and power in the hands of the industrialists contributed to the view of the late 1800s as the "Gilded Age." The name was first given to this period by Mark Twain and Charles Dudley Warner. In 1873, they published *The Gilded Age*, a novel intended to ridicule Americans who were rushing to "get rich quick." The term came to represent the contrast between the glittery surface of the American way of life and the ruthless, money-driven decisions that fueled economic expansion.

Monopolies

A monopoly exists when a single company or group controls a product or service. In order to establish a monopoly, a company usually has to control the resource needed to produce the product and have sole control over the process used to produce the product. Or it needs permission from the government to be the only producer of the product. Public utilities, such as electricity, are considered monopolies because the government allows only certain companies to provide these vital public services. The postal service is also considered a legal monopoly and is heavily regulated by the government.

The robber barons were accused of establishing private monopolies at the expense of the American people. The Sherman Antitrust Act was created in response to this. In 1911, the Standard Oil Company was finally broken up under the Act. In 1999 and 2000, the United States government used the Sherman Antitrust Act to question the tactics of Microsoft, a huge computer corporation. It accused Microsoft of being a monopoly because it controlled which products and services computer manufacturers could feature on their machines. Microsoft had been requiring computer manufacturers to use its own Internet services if they wanted to use the software also produced by the company. That requirement was shutting out the Internet services of other companies. The Department of Justice decided Microsoft should be divided into three smaller organizations. The company is fighting that decision in an appeal that could take years.

The American Workforce

Before the Civil War, family farms employed most people. But by 1870, there were 12 cities in the United States with populations of more than 100,000. The nature of employment changed, as people went to work for the owners of large industries. They became employees whose working conditions, hours, and output were all controlled by managers.

The Building and Mining Industries

It was the rapid expansion of cities and factories that caused this great change in where and how people worked. The urban growth of the 1800s required large amounts of lumber for housing and industrial buildings. Lumber companies sprang up, employing thousands of people. The supply of trees appeared endless, but forests rapidly began to disappear. And, just as wood was needed for the buildings, stone was needed for foundations and streets. Public buildings were now also being built with stone. Stone quarries, like the lumber companies, were established in areas where their resources were available, employing workers by the thousands.

Energy was needed to heat new homes and run new machinery, and so coal production increased to meet this demand. It took over 3,000 pounds (1,360 kg) of coal just to heat one home during a typical winter in the Northeast. In the United States, the largest coal reserves were in a region called the Appalachian field which included parts of Alabama, Kentucky, Ohio, Pennsylvania, Tennessee, Virginia, and West Virginia. The coal deposits were found in large veins often running deep in the ground.

Coal Mining

Coal mining was a difficult way to make a living. Each day, miners would work in underground mines, often stooped over for hours at a time. As they dug out the coal, coal dust would fill the air, covering the miners with a thick black film and filling their lungs. Accidents were frequent and often deadly. There was little compensation for these working conditions, as wages were low.

Young boys were used as "breakers," to pick rock debris out of the coal. Just like the adult miners, they worked long hours and barely made enough money to survive. Thousands of boys were killed or permanently injured in accidents each year.

The conditions of the settlements around the coal mines were also tragic. The waste products produced through mining would build up near the mines and run down through the towns. Coal dust also settled on streets, homes, and water supplies.

These breaker boys and men were photographed in 1891 in the Kohinore coal mine in Shenandoah, Pennsylvania.

By 1900, three-quarters of a million men and boys labored in mines for the growing coal companies. In the mines, each man acted independently. He agreed on his wage with the mine operator, used his own tools, and could even bring in extra laborers if he had been certified as a "skilled miner."

Iron and Steel Production

Until the 1860s, the steel being made was not sufficiently refined to be used for machinery or building. But as steel processes improved, stronger steel was produced that could be used for heavy machinery and for structural purposes.

By 1890, the iron and steel business was the fastest-growing industry in the country. More than a million workers toiled to produce half the world's supply of these products. Much of the steel produced was greedily consumed by the still-expanding railroad industry. As the country rushed to build a network of rail lines, iron and steel were needed for the rails, the rail cars, and railroad bridges.

The conditions in the steel plants were in some ways much better than those in the coal fields. The work was hot and dangerous and accidents were frequent, but steel companies were fiercely competitive. They often improved working conditions in order to increase production, and the workers benefited from the improvements. For example, Andrew Carnegie was one of the first to introduce an eight-hour day in his factories, rather than demanding that people work unlimited hours or lose their jobs.

The Growth of Factories

The invention of the power loom in the early 1800s had made the textile industry one of the first successes of the Industrial Age. The industry expanded even more during the Civil War to provide cloth for military uniforms and clothing. After the war, many of the mills were successfully converted to the production of textiles for civilian clothing, bedding, and household goods. By 1900, almost 1.5 million workers were employed in the mills.

In 1860, the major industrial center of the United States was in the Northeastern states where most of the textile mills were situated. By 1900, industry had expanded into the Midwest, due largely to the growth of the iron and steel industry.

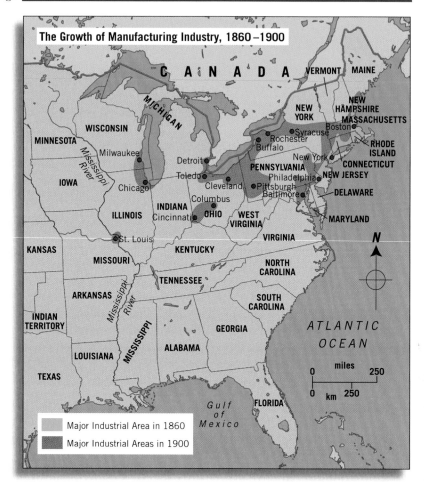

The Growth of Manufacturing Industry, 1860–1900

Major Industrial Area in 1860
Major Industrial Areas in 1900

In addition, food processing was moving off farms and into factories. With the growth of railroads, it became profitable to package food in factories for shipment across the country. In Minnesota, Charles A. Pillsbury discovered a new method to mill wheat. By 1883, he had built the largest mill in the country. The development of the refrigerated rail car in the 1860s enabled meat to be shipped all over the United States.

By 1890, nearly a quarter of a million workers labored to produce meat, grain, and vegetable products. Often, they were concentrated in specific areas. Illinois, for example, led all other states in packing and distributing beef and other meat products. Minnesota, with Pillsbury's mill, became the leading flour-producing state.

Printing businesses, alcoholic beverage producers, and the chemical industry all experienced growth fueled by the increasing demand for their products. In the Northeast, and to some extent in the West and South, factories needed a constant supply of labor.

The New Workforce

Even though the hours were long and the work backbreaking, millions of Americans rushed to join the growing industrial workforce. By the turn of the century, there were over 30 million industrial workers in the United States.

Men, women, and children labored six or seven days a week, working between 60 and 80 hours. The government did little to regulate working conditions. Most people earned ten cents an hour or less and could be laid off at any time. Often, factories had inadequate ventilation and poor lighting. The few restrooms provided were insanitary and crowded. If workers were injured on the job, they weren't paid while they recovered. If they died from an injury at work, workers' families rarely received benefits from the employer. Industrial accidents were common: By some estimates, as many as 25,000 workers were killed in factories each year. Thousands more were injured.

Workers leave a New England factory after work in this painting by Winslow Homer. In the Northeast, and increasingly in the West and South, the American workforce moved out of agricultural labor and into the factories. Men, women, and children toiled long hours for little pay.

Children commonly worked in factories and mines. They earned very little money, and every cent was desperately needed by their families. Entire families had to work just to achieve sufficient shelter, food, and clothing. Depending on the needs of the family, children went to work as soon as they were able, often before the age of ten.

Providing Services

Until the mid-1800s, most women worked in their homes or on family farms. By 1890, nearly 4 million women had joined the industrial workforce. Most were employed in factories, but a few women began to find work in professions, such as medicine and law, that were once considered exclusively male.

Sweatshops

The clothing, or garment, industry strove to keep up with the demand for clothes. "Garment districts" appeared in New York City and other urban centers. These districts included factories turning out suits, dresses, and other garments. But the factories could not fill the demand, and so within these districts, sweatshops, or small workshops, also appeared.

Sweatshops employed mostly immigrants, especially women and children, to cut and assemble garments. The conditions were terrible. Cramped and crowded buildings were common, and some sweatshops were just the homes of the workers. Immigrants labored six days a week, often for 12 hours a day.

They were paid a few dollars a week as long as there was work. At first, most garment workers came from Germany and Ireland. However, by 1900, over 70 percent were immigrant Jews from Eastern Europe.

A pant maker's sweatshop in New York's garment district, photographed by social reformer Jacob Riis. The total weekly income of the immigrant family seen here was $8.

Other women worked in the offices that were cropping up to support the growing needs of large companies. Accountants, lawyers, and other businessmen established their companies in cities around the country. Beginning around 1870, women began entering office work in large numbers. They enjoyed a relatively clean working environment and higher wages than women in factories. They had a professional status because of the skilled duties they performed. The growing use of the typewriter in the 1870s soon led to secretarial training and even more office work for women.

Some workers were self-employed. City people had to buy most of their daily needs, and this resulted in the growth of street peddlers. Products such as ice, fresh meats and vegetables, dairy products, and coal were sold by these vendors who traveled door-to-door in horse-drawn wagons or set up stands in the busy streets. Shopkeepers were barely able to stay ahead of demand as consumers required more textiles, grains, and other domestic goods. Blacksmiths were needed, not just to shoe horses or build plows, but to turn out the vast number of pots, pans, nails, and other household goods needed by a growing number of families.

The first successful typewriter was developed in Milwaukee, Wisconsin, in 1868. The invention led to a huge increase in the number of female office employees, such as this woman using a typewriter in 1872.

The Early Labor Movement

As industry grew and industrialists got richer, most workers remained poor. One of the reasons that big businesses like the railroad industry, mining companies, and textile factories could keep workers under terrible conditions was that workers had trouble uniting with one another. Many immigrant groups did not get involved with each other, and blacks and whites were segregated to a large extent. Men and women did not often work together either.

> "Our organization . . . does not control the production of the world. That is controlled by the employers. . . . I look first to the trade I represent . . ."
>
> *Adolph Strasser, president of the Cigarmakers' Union, 1883*

Nevertheless, the long hours, low pay, and huge differences between conditions for the rich and poor led to dissatisfaction among workers. Their unhappiness was also caused by the growing number of immigrants flooding into the country. Often, out of desperation, immigrants were prepared to work for even lower wages and in even worse conditions than native-born Americans. As the number of immigrants grew and American workers were displaced by cheaper immigrant labor, American-born workers began to fear for their jobs.

Early attempts to bring workers together in labor unions, or groups of workers that fought for improved conditions, met with little success. Social reformers tried to organize workers to unite so that they could push for shorter working hours, better workplaces, and decent wages. In 1873, the Workingmen's Benevolent Association, a miners' union, attempted to wage a strike, which is a form of protest where workers stop work in an attempt to force employers to meet their demands. However, workers in fear of losing their jobs refused to take part. Shoemakers tried to unite under the name of the Knights of St. Crispin, but that, too, met with little enthusiasm from workers.

The Growth of Unions

One union that did survive was the Noble Order of the Knights of Labor, which was formed as a secret society in 1869 by a small group of garment workers. Over the next few years, the group expanded to include factory workers, miners, ironworkers, stonemasons and others. By 1878, the union had 9,000 members. The Knights began to push for an eight-hour day, equal wages for women, and limitations on the use of child labor.

In 1881, at a meeting in Pittsburgh, representatives from several unions founded the Federation of Organized Trades and Labor Unions. (Trades unions were mostly for skilled workers or craftsmen, whereas labor unions represented mainly industrial and unskilled laborers.) It was not powerful

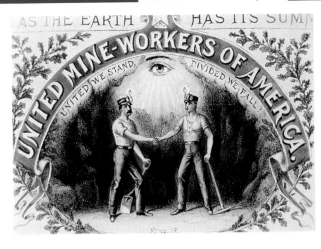

enough effectively to unite the separate unions, but on September 5, 1882, nearly 5,000 workers came together. Carpenters, brick masons, iron workers, and other laborers marched in the first Labor Day parade in New York City. The parade was organized by the New York Central Labor Union to protest the long working hours for non-government workers. In the 1840s, legislation had guaranteed an eight-hour workday to federal government workers, but employees in private companies had no such limit on their working day.

This emblem for the United Mine Workers sums up the attitude of working people toward their employers with the slogan, "United We Stand, Divided We Fall." As more and more workers moved into industries controlled by the powerful robber barons, the unions slowly found a voice in the workplace.

Strikes, Successes, and Failures

In 1884, the Knights of Labor organized strikes against the Union Pacific Railroad after the railroad cut wages. They were successful in forcing the company to reinstate the higher wages. The following year, they organized a strike against the Erie Railroad. Again, they were successful. By 1885, their membership had increased to nearly three-quarters of a million workers.

Other workers began to follow their example. In March 1885, railroad workers struck against a cut in wages at the Missouri Pacific Railroad. Again, management surrendered, but more importantly, it began to recognize the union as the formal representative of the workers.

In 1894, George Pullman reduced wages at his Pullman Company plant in Illinois, but did not cut the rent for the workers living in his houses. Tension mounted and resulted in the Pullman Strike. The strikers were led by Eugene V. Debs, who had organized the American Railroad Union in 1893. Railroad workers refused to handle any trains that included Pullman cars and since most trains included these, the strike soon spread throughout the country. At one point, 60,000 railroad workers participated in the strike.

"While there is a lower class, I am in it. While there is a criminal class, I am of it. While there is a soul in prison, I am not free."

Eugene Debs, Labor and Freedom

On July 4, 1894, federal troops entered Chicago's railroad yards to break a strike of thousands of railroad workers. The workers were striking in sympathy with the Pullman Company employees who were protesting a cut in wages. By the time the strike ended on August 3, there had been 13 people killed and 53 wounded in Chicago.

The Pullman Company called on the federal government to help. Attorney General Richard Olney declared that the strike was interfering with mail delivery and ordered it to cease. President Cleveland sent troops to preserve order and had Debs arrested and sent to jail for contempt of court. The strike was broken.

The Haymarket Bombing

As union groups began to organize, they developed strength in numbers. On May 1, 1886, The Knights of Labor called a strike. They demanded an eight-hour workday and a wage of $2 per day for their members. On May 3, striking workers from the McCormick Reaper Company in Chicago attacked strikebreakers, the people at their factory who continued to go to work during the strike. The police were called in, a riot broke out, and six people were killed by police.

The following day, on May 4, 1886, thousands of people came together at Haymarket Square in Chicago to protest the police killings. The city, fearing more violence, sent in 180 police officers. Someone threw a bomb at the police and seven officers were killed. Police and city officials blamed the labor leaders, claiming they were anarchists, meaning people who sought to overthrow the government. Several of the labor activists were arrested, tried, and convicted. The leaders were hanged and others sent to prison for life. Newspapers across the country carried the story, and it became clear that many people were afraid of the unions and the union bosses.

The affair ruined the Knights of Labor. Before the Haymarket Bombing, their numbers had reached 750,000 and their influence was rising. Just four years later, their membership had dropped below 100,000.

As the influence of the Knights declined, another group rose to take its place. Several small trades unions asked that the Knights stop taking craftsmen as members where unions for their trades already existed. The Knights refused the demand. In December 1886, representatives from several crafts met in Columbus, Ohio, to organize the new American Federation of Labor (AF of L). Samuel Gompers, president of the Cigarmakers' Union, was elected the first AF of L president. For the next several years, the Knights of Labor and the AF of L spent most of their time fighting with one another over representation of various crafts and trades.

On May 4, 1886, as labor activist Samuel Fielden spoke to a crowd of workers in Haymarket Square, Chicago, a bomb exploded. It was thrown into a group of about 180 police officers who had come to break up the rally. The fatal explosion turned public opinion against strikers and unions.

Samuel Gompers (1850–1924)

Samuel Gompers was born in London. He only attended school for four years before being apprenticed to a cigarmaker. In 1863, his family emigrated to New York City where he continued to work in the cigarmaking industry. Gompers became active in the labor movement of the city's Lower East Side through his membership in the Cigarmakers' Union. By 1874, he was president of that group.

In 1886, Gompers was chosen as the first president of the American Federation of Labor, an office he would hold for 38 years. Gompers believed the purpose of labor unions was to push for better working conditions such as shorter workdays, higher wages, and improved workplaces. He did not want to be part of a political process, nor did he wish to expand his union's mission beyond the labor needs of the workers. For instance, he did not believe unions should commit themselves to any political party. Because he kept the AF of L focused on labor issues, rather than on politics, Gompers was able to strengthen his union while other unions failed.

During World War I, Gompers encouraged workers to unite behind the war effort by organizing the War Committee on Labor. Gompers was still president of the AF of L when he died in 1924.

The Homestead Strike

The Homestead Mill in Homestead, Pennsylvania, was part of the Carnegie Steel empire. Workers there belonged to the Amalgamated Association of Iron and Steel Workers of America. Henry Clay Frick was chairman of the Carnegie Steel Company, and had little use for the union. In 1892, union members requested a wage increase, but Frick was trying to cut wages instead. He was also trying to reduce the influence of the union.

The union workers voted to strike. Frick responded by bringing in 300 security guards from the Pinkerton Detective Agency. As the barges carrying the security force arrived, shots were fired from the crowd of steel and iron workers waiting at the dock. The security force surrendered after the attack killed seven of its men and injured many more. The Governor of Pennsylvania ordered troops into the area, but before they arrived, Frick himself was shot and stabbed in his office. Although his injuries were not serious, the tide of public sympathy turned away from striking workers and began to support management.

Labor Unions

In the early days of the Industrial Age in America, employers often set working conditions with each individual employee. Because a single worker had little bargaining power with a factory, workers began banding together into organized trades unions to demand better working conditions. Farmers in rural areas also banded together in alliances in order to purchase supplies in greater bulk and at better prices, to share the costs of equipment, and to gain economic power.

Legislation protecting the rights of workers began being passed by the states and the federal government during the nineteenth century. Such legislation guaranteed minimum wages, established working hours, and sometimes provided benefits in case of accident, sickness, or death on the job. Federal and state laws also guaranteed workers the right to establish unions and set negotiating procedures with their employers.

Traditionally, unions have represented workers who produce goods rather than services. Unions reached their greatest bargaining power in the late 1960s and the 1970s when manufacturing was driving the economy. Workers joined unions in record numbers and union representatives drove hard bargains with employers. Strikes were common, especially in the automobile and shipping industries. Since the mid-1980s, however, the service industry has grown, and so union membership and the power of the unions have declined.

Immigrants and City Life

By 1880, there were over 50 million people living in the United States. Nearly 7 million of them had been born elsewhere, and the country was about to experience another wave of immigration. In the 1870s, for example, about 2.7 million immigrants arrived on American soil. During the 1880s, that figure was well over 5 million.

The New Wave of Immigrants

Before the Civil War, most immigrants to America were from Western Europe. This trend continued in the 1880s, when two-thirds of those arriving came from Britain, Ireland, Germany, and Scandinavia. As industrialization spread across Western Europe, however, many people there chose to stay in their native countries and the nature of emigration to the United States began to change. Over the next two decades, increasingly large numbers of immigrants to the eastern United States came from Russia, Italy, and Austria-Hungary. In the West, Chinese immigrants arrived by the thousands.

Thousands of people in those countries had heard wonderful stories about the United States. Many, including European Jews, had been persecuted for their religious beliefs in their homelands. They were hoping to find religious freedom in America. Although some family groups arrived, most of the immigrants were men and boys, and nearly all were poor and had little education. They worked and saved, sometimes for years, in order to bring the rest of their family over. Others worked in America simply to make enough money so they could return to their homeland and survive there.

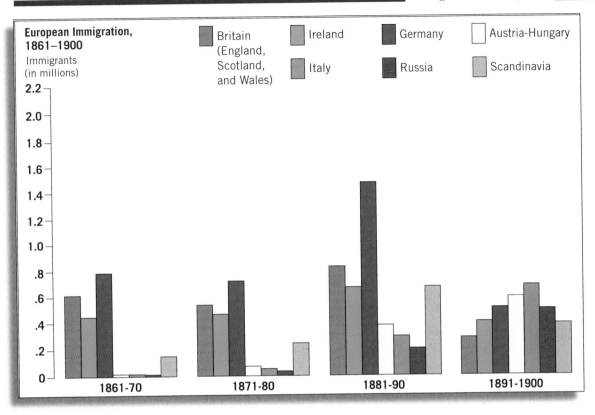

European Immigration, 1861–1900

Immigrants (in millions)

Legend: Britain (England, Scotland, and Wales) · Ireland · Germany · Austria-Hungary · Italy · Russia · Scandinavia

Years: 1861-70, 1871-80, 1881-90, 1891-1900

A New Life in a New Land

Those arriving in the United States in the late 1800s wanted to blend into the culture as quickly as they could. Most people sought to adopt the American way of life, recognizing that it was the best way to get ahead. Yet many could not read or write, and most could not speak English. They often arrived knowing no one, and there was no government welfare system to support them. Many of them settled in New York, Hartford, Boston, and other east coast cities.

Immigrants crowded together in ghettos, the neighborhoods of large cities where people from one particular country clustered together. They learned of Andrew Carnegie, John D. Rockefeller, and others who were born poor, had little education, but attained success and vast wealth. It was this possibility that drove and motivated millions to learn English, adopt American customs, work long hours in factories, and raise their children to be Americans.

This chart shows how the pattern of immigration to the United States changed between the 1860s and 1900. From 1861 to 1890, most immigrants were British, Irish, and German, as they had been before the Civil War. In the 1890s, Western European immigration declined and people from Russia, Austria-Hungary, and Italy came in larger numbers.

Ellis Island

By the late 1880s, Castle Garden, the office of New York's Commissioners of Emigration in Manhattan, was overflowing with people coming to the United States from other countries. Castle Garden was closed in 1890, and the federal government opened its own immigration office in New York City. On New Year's Day, 1892, that office was moved from Battery Park to Ellis Island, located in New York Bay. It quickly became the busiest immigration station in the country, often processing 5,000 people each day.

As immigrants disembarked at Ellis Island, they were forced to wait in long lines, sometimes for hours, until they could be processed. Their passports and other papers were checked, and they were given a health examination. After processing, they were free to go. Because they had little or no money, most settled not far from where they entered the country.

By 1947, nearly 20 million immigrants had passed through Ellis Island, but those numbers were declining. In 1954, Ellis Island was officially closed and the service was transferred to a new office in Manhattan.

A group of European arrivals waiting on Ellis Island to be transported into New York City.

Some were able to achieve their dreams in the United States because, unlike the societies many immigrants left, there was nothing confining them to the ghettos. When financially able, they were free to move out of the slums to better apartments in neighborhoods where their children could receive good education and greater opportunity. For most immigrants, it was the combination of a strong economy and their own determination that allowed them to do this.

The Immigrant Workforce

Immigrants were also willing to do work that many Americans did not want to do. American-born workers had a greater choice of employment than immigrants had. White, American-born women entering the workforce could find office work, and men could become supervisors and trained engineers in the growing industries. And as these Americans filled the professional jobs, the low paid, unskilled labor was left to immigrants. The jobs fell into three main categories: sweatshops, factories, and agriculture.

Another employment avenue for newly-arrived immigrants was domestic work. The growing wealth of the middle class in America meant they had more time and money. Because middle-class Americans wanted to engage in leisure activities, they were willing to pay for servants. Immigrants became the chief source of labor for this domestic market.

Immigrants from Europe, like this group walking along Broadway in New York City in about 1880, often arrived with no work and nowhere to live. Most moved into city ghettos, the ethnic neighborhoods where Russians, Italians, or Irish lived among others from their own countries.

The Strain on Cities

Even before the boom in immigration, American cities were becoming crowded and overburdened. Immigration added to the social problems even though it had not caused them. The

growing population quickly put cities under even greater pressure and a shortage of housing developed. As available property became more scarce, the cost of buildings and land skyrocketed. Dishonest builders constructed cheap, unsafe housing which was rapidly filled with new city dwellers. Immigrants lived in crowded apartments in slum neighborhoods. Children who had been abandoned could be found living on the street, sleeping in makeshift shacks and boxes.

Services lagged behind, too. Garbage removal services could not keep up with the amount of waste being discarded. Fires in cities burned out of control as fire departments were overwhelmed. Streets grew with the construction of new buildings, but city crews could not pave them quickly enough. Instead, they were rough, dirty thoroughfares where crime and disease flourished. Sewerage systems and water pumping stations were not sufficient to meet the demand. Drinking water became unfit to consume and in many cities, sewage ran openly into streets, streams, and rivers.

This alley off Mulberry Street in New York City was known as "Bandit's Roost." The area was infamous for its criminal activities. This photograph was taken by Jacob Riis, whose record of life among the immigrants of the Lower East Side shocked many.

"People will not live on the farm as they seemed willing to do a hundred years ago."

James Bryce, historian, 1895

Anti-Immigrant Feeling

When problems arose in the cities, immigrants found themselves blamed by native-born Americans. As the number of Catholics and Jews continued to rise, Protestants felt threatened by the practice of these religions in their communities. Chinese and Japanese immigrants incited fear because of their different race and Asian culture. And the fact that immigrants were willing to work for lower pay angered many American workers.

The "Yellow Peril"

Although much of the concern about immigration took place in the cities of the Northeast, the West also had an immigrant boom. Beginning in 1854, thousands of Chinese immigrants came to the United States to work as laborers on the transcontinental railroads. In the first year, about 13,000 workers arrived, and by 1868, there were 75,000 Chinese in America Between 1868 and 1882, another 160,000 Chinese arrived. The vast majority of the immigrants were men without their families.

Tension mounted after the railroad construction was complete, when the Chinese began competing with American-born workers for other jobs. Another problem was that the Chinese did not melt into the American culture as other groups tried to do. Their Asian way of life was different, and they often kept their own language and customs.

Chinese immigrants were frequent victims of robberies and assaults simply because they looked different from other Americans. As anti-Chinese feelings grew, riots broke out in 1877. Americans began talking about the "yellow peril," because the Chinese were often referred to as being yellow rather than white or black. Some Americans pushed Congress to take action. Finally, in 1882, a year in which nearly 40,000 Chinese immigrants arrived, Congress passed a law called the Chinese Exclusion Act. This completely banned Chinese immigration to the United States. The law was written to be in effect for ten years, but it was eventually extended until 1943.

The immigrants themselves were often surprised by what they found in America. They worked long hours at hard labor just to make enough money to eat and live. Their working conditions were unsafe, and their children often had to quit school to help support the family. Their housing situations were usually unhealthy and they had little or no access to medical assistance. It was not the new life they had hoped for.

As immigrants filled the cities, many wealthier Americans responded by leaving. They moved to the outskirts of town to distance themselves from the poverty, disease, and lack of sanitary conditions. Throughout the 1880s and 1890s, public

> "America is God's crucible, the great Melting Pot where all the races . . . are melting and reforming."
>
> *Israel Zangwill, writer*

opinion built up against the "open-door" immigration policy that had allowed nearly unlimited numbers of immigrants into the country. American workers feared for their jobs. Social workers who tried to provide medical and housing assistance to immigrants felt they would be unable to meet the vast needs of the ever-growing immigrant population. Economists began to worry about the long-term effects of immigration on the country's economic strength.

There was growing political support for a literacy, or reading, requirement as a way to control the immigrants arriving in America. In other words, no one should be allowed to come into the country unless he or she could read. Congress even passed a literacy bill in 1896, but President Cleveland vetoed it, believing it to be out of character with the history of the country.

Corruption in the Cities

Many local politicians used the pressure in the cities to increase their own wealth and power. Rather than working to solve the cities' problems, they would gain votes by buying and selling favors within local communities. Behind the scenes, political leaders controlled much of what went on in the city. Often, they were associated with societies or clubs which they used as their power bases to build political support among voters.

One such group in New York City, known as Tammany Hall (named after a Delaware Indian Chief), was made up of New York Democrats. Tammany Hall was divided into 13 tribes. The group used Indian names to represent the officers and referred to their meeting places as wigwams. The club worked hard to gain the trust of the poor in the city: factory workers, immigrants, and soldiers who had returned to New York following the Civil War. The club would "help" these citizens by finding them jobs and housing, supporting their labor unions and churches, and providing information and services. In return, those who had received the favors would vote the Tammany leaders into public office.

William Marcy Tweed (1823–78)

Tweed was born in New York City. He became a bookkeeper, but was also active in the city's politics. Tweed was a New York City alderman from 1852 to 1853, and then was elected to Congress where he served until 1855. By 1857, he was a central figure in the Tammany Hall group. Over the next 14 years, Tweed held a number of city and state jobs, including Director of Public Works, which he used to further his own political power and to increase his personal wealth.

SHERIFF'S OFFICE
OF THE CITY AND COUNTY OF NEW YORK.

December 6th, 1875.

$10,000 Reward.

The above reward will be paid for the apprehension and delivery to the undersigned, or his proper agents, of

WM. M. TWEED,

Who escaped from the Jailor of the City and County of New York, on Saturday, December 4th, 1875. At the time of his escape he was under indictment for Forgery and other crimes, and was under arrest in civil actions in which bail had been fixed by the Court at the amount of Four Million Dollars.

The following is a Description of said WM. M. TWEED:

He is about fifty-five years of age, about five feet eleven inches high, will weigh about two hundred and eighty pounds, very portly, ruddy complexion, has rather large, coarse, prominent features and large prominent nose; rather small blue or grey eyes, grey hair, from originally auburn color; head nearly bald on top from forehead back to crown, and bare part of ruddy color; head projecting toward the crown. His beard may be removed or dyed, and he may wear a wig or be otherwise disguised. His photograph is attached.

WILLIAM C. CONNER,
Sheriff.

The wanted poster issued for William Tweed after he escaped from jail in 1875.

Tweed's level of corruption was breathtaking. He received money from businessmen who wanted construction or other business contracts with the City. He also took money from land sales he arranged. Unions and other groups paid Tweed to do favors for them; and he bribed voters and corrupted judges.

Tweed's greed and misdeeds caught up with him in the end. In 1871, Samuel Tilden, a local Democrat who would later become governor of New York, turned in Tweed because he felt the "Boss" had cut him out of a deal. Although he escaped to Spain, the Spanish authorities returned Tweed to the United States and he finally died in prison.

One of the most famous leaders of Tammany Hall was William Marcy "Boss" Tweed, the director of New York's Department of Public Works. In this position, he was able to charge the city for building works and services that had not been provided and for rents on properties that did not exist. The money went into the pockets of the "Tammany Ring,"

WHO STOLE THE PEOPLE'S MONEY ? — DO TELL . N.Y.TIMES.   'TWAS HIM.

The cartoonist Thomas Nast used his skill to make repeated attacks on the corruption of the "Tweed Ring." This cartoon shows members of the ring passing the blame until it reaches William Tweed (front left).

or "Tweed Ring," as the group was also known. It has been estimated that Tweed and his ring swindled between $30 million and $200 million out of the city. In July 1871, *The New York Times* published an article about Tammany Hall's activities. A few months later, Tweed was arrested and convicted of embezzlement and corruption.

Social Reforms

Around 1890, the tide began to turn. Social reformers who were concerned with the plight of the poor in the cities began to fight back against the local political bosses. Through newspapers, magazine articles, and word of mouth, the social reformers brought to light the corruption that was occurring. Over time, they broke down the political machines that the local politicians had built.

Certain newspaper journalists began to call attention, not just to corruption in the cities, but to the problems created by poverty. One of the most notable of these was the photographer Jacob Riis, who worked as a reporter for the New York *Tribune*. Riis led other journalists in a reform movement demanding decent living conditions for poor people and the enforcement of housing regulations.

Jacob August Riis (1849–1914)

Riis was born in Ribe, Denmark. In 1870, he came to the United States where he worked as a carpenter. For several years, Riis lived the life of an extremely poor immigrant in New York City until, in 1877, he got a job as a reporter on police matters for the New York *Tribune* newspaper. His office was on the Lower East Side, in the midst of the immigrant ghettos.

Riis spent nights walking through the slums, recording life in the underbelly of the city and photographing whatever he could. He used his position as a journalist and his remarkable photographs to bring to public attention the plight of New York's poor. In 1890, Riis published his findings in a book called *How the Other Half Lives*. The impact of the book was immediate and intense. It showed people firsthand the unhealthy, filthy, living conditions endured by most poor immigrants in the cities.

Theodore Roosevelt, at the time the New York City police commissioner, was so moved by the book that he supported Riis's efforts to reform slum housing and improve local schools. Riis also backed the development of playgrounds and parks in city neighborhoods.

By the late 1880s, there were several wealthy young people who were concerned about the living conditions of urban immigrants. Some of them organized "settlement houses," which were located in the poorest neighborhoods and provided assistance and services to the poor. The first of these, Hull House, was started by Jane Addams and Ellen Gates Starr in Chicago in 1889, to help solve the social and housing problems in the city. Hull House taught classes in cooking and sewing, as well as in music, art, and theater. It included a gymnasium, a nursery, and numerous social activities such as dances and parties. The model established at Hull House was copied in other cities, including Boston and New York.

Politicians could no longer ignore the plight of poor working people and immigrants in the ghettos. They began to introduce regulations to improve working conditions. In 1842, Massachusetts had limited the workday in factories to ten hours a day for children under the age of 12. In the late 1800s, other states slowly followed suit. Some states limited hours for women and children, and a few regulated hours for some male workers, but the laws often were not enforced.

City officials began to look at living conditions in the poorer urban districts. From the 1870s to 1900, Boston spent nearly one-third of the city's funds on improving the water supply, and on sewerage and other sanitation projects. New York, Chicago, Philadelphia, and other large cities also tried to keep pace with water and sanitation projects. In 1901, New York passed laws that set standards for bathrooms and decent ventilation in homes, and for the amount of open space that had to be set aside in the city.

While these were steps in the right direction, they were inadequate to meet fully the needs of immigrants and other poor urban dwellers. And, too often, the laws continued to be broken by dishonest local politicians.

As people began to fight against unfair working conditions, this group of child workers from a textile mill went on strike in 1890. One of their signs read, "More School Less Hospital," which refers to the large number of accidents suffered by children in dangerous factories.

The Statue of Liberty

In 1886, France gave the United States a gift that has since become a symbol of the freedom offered to immigrants arriving on American shores. To celebrate the 100th anniversary of American independence and the friendship between the two countries, the French government commissioned sculptor Frederic Bartholdi to design a statue called "Liberty Enlightening the World."

The statue was built of copper sheets attached to an iron frame. One of the world's largest statues, the figure reaches 152 feet (46 m) toward the sky. Because of its size and weight of 290 tons (254 metric tons), Liberty had to be taken apart before being shipped to the United States. It was placed in New York Harbor and dedicated by President Cleveland in a ceremony on October 28, 1886.

In 1903, the words of poet Emma Lazarus were inscribed on the pedestal:

"Give me your tired, your poor,
Your huddled masses yearning to breathe free,
The wretched refuse of your teeming shore.
Send these, the homeless, tempest-tost to me,
I lift my lamp beside the golden door."

As the statue neared its 100th birthday, it underwent a three-year restoration. The iron framework was replaced with stainless steel and the copper sheeting was refinished. The original torch, made from glass and metal, was replaced with one of gilded copper.

Changes in Farming and the South

A griculture had long been the backbone of America's economy, and in the late 1800s, the number of farms continued to rise. In 1860, there were 2 million farms; by 1890, that number had more than doubled. The rural population, which was feeding the fast-growing urban population, increased from 25 million to over 40 million people, and food production increased with the number of farmers. Cotton production, an essential part of the Southern economy, grew from 5 million bales to 8.5 million bales annually. American exports also doubled during the period and nearly 75 percent of these exports consisted of agricultural products.

The Agricultural Economy

In spite of all this, the agricultural way of life waned as manufacturing industries grew in influence and size. During the same time period, the urban population grew fourfold and industry was expanding at a far greater rate than farming. No longer was the United States economy driven only by agriculture.

Immediately after the Civil War, farmers had enjoyed strong demand and high prices, but during the 1880s prices fell. Following the war, cotton brought 31 cents a pound. By 1893, it was only bringing 6 cents a pound. The price of corn went from 75 cents a bushel in 1869 down to 28 cents a bushel 20 years later. At the same time, farmers' costs were rising. They had to pay whatever the railroads and grain storage companies demanded for moving and storing their produce.

The economic decline did not affect all farmers in the same way. At first, the South was somewhat protected from declining prices, in part because the farms there were established and did not require cash resources to buy equipment or land. In time, however, the newer farms in the Midwest and on the Plains began to do better. The soil was fertile, there were several years of good rainfall, and there was a seemingly limitless supply of farmland. In the South, on the other hand, the rainfall was not as plentiful, much of the land had been overworked, and labor was more difficult to find. Southern farmers began to suffer the greatest losses.

After the Civil War, black people in the South were no longer slaves, but they still had few opportunities. Many, like these cotton laborers in about 1870, were unable to acquire their own land and continued to work for white plantation owners.

The Mechanization of Farming

Even though the influence of the agricultural community was declining, it was still a vital part of the American economy. As the railroad system expanded, new markets were established for farmers. In the late 1800s, another significant change took place: the mechanization of the American farm. By 1890, nearly a thousand businesses were producing farming equipment and farmers bought it as quickly as they could.

Dairy farming was revolutionized by several inventions. The dairy centrifuge allowed farmers to separate cream from milk mechanically, lowering the cost of dairy products. A new machine was invented that could measure the fat content of milk. This allowed dairies to establish standards for the contents of dairy products. Improvements to harvesting equipment lowered the cost of grain production. New chemical combinations provided more effective fertilizers that enriched the soil and increased crop yields.

Tenant Farming and Sharecropping

In 1880, a government report showed that one out of four farms was operated by tenants, or people who rented the land from landowners. In the South, the landlord and tenant usually entered into share contracts, or the sharecropping system. Sharecroppers were often black farmers who had no chance of making enough money to buy their own land.

The share contracts usually lasted a year. Under the contract, a landowner would provide the land. Sometimes he also provided housing and the equipment and supplies needed to farm the land. There was no one formula for sharecropping. If the tenant contributed just the labor, he would typically give the owner 75 percent of the crop. If he contributed to the cost of the equipment or supplies, then he kept more of the harvest.

Because sharecroppers were so poor, they often promised a share of their crop to local merchants in exchange for food or other living supplies. Unfortunately, that meant there was little left for the sharecropper when all others had taken their share. Sharecropping was rarely a successful system for the tenant, and about one-third of the tenants moved on each year. Others took second jobs just to make ends meet.

Farmers' Alliances

Farms in different parts of the country specialized in particular products. The South produced most of the rice, cotton, sugar, and tobacco harvested in the United States. Upper sections of the South (Virginia, Maryland, Kentucky, and Tennessee) also produced millions of bushels of wheat, corn, and other grains, but it was in the Midwest that grain production really took hold. The availability of open land led to the creation of large farms that covered thousands or even tens of thousands of acres. By 1890, they had become the prominent producers of corn and wheat. Western farmers also became leaders in livestock production and in dairy farming. Food manufacturing industries in the region, such as cereal makers, soon followed.

As farming expanded successfully in the Midwest and on the Great Plains, the South suffered. Out of frustration,

Southern farmers began to band together, informally at first, into associations or alliances. In 1867, Oliver Kelley had founded the Patrons of Husbandry, an organization that provided social contacts for rural families. Members became known as "Grangers" and local chapters as "Granges." The group took hold between 1872 and 1874, during which time 14,000 Granges were created.

It wasn't long before the alliances became more official. The Grangers became active in fighting the railroads over lower freight prices for transporting farm produce. Another group, the Knights of Reliance, formed in Texas in 1877. Because of the advantages of working cooperatively, the group quickly spread throughout Texas and then into other Southern states. The Knights of Reliance purchased supplies in bulk and redistributed them to its members.

Like the Grangers, other local alliances, such as the Agricultural Wheel, the Southern Alliance, and the Northern Alliance, had been established for social reasons. As prices of farm produce began to decline in the mid-1880s, these alliances also turned their attention to economic and political activities.

The Populist Movement

The alliances began to band together to increase their power. The groups campaigned on political issues, backed specific candidates in elections, and gained control of eight Southern state legislatures. On the national level, 47 congressmen and senators were elected on alliance-sponsored platforms. But because both Republicans and Democrats refused completely to endorse the alliance movement, alliance leaders began to push for the creation of a new, third party.

In 1892, alliance leaders met in St. Louis, Missouri, with representatives of the Knights of Labor and nearly 1,000 other reformers. Together, they organized the Populist, or People's, party and planned a national convention in Omaha, Nebraska, in July. The party favored several reforms. One was the introduction of a graduated income tax on citizens.

"It is no longer a government of the people, by the people, and for the people, but a government of Wall Street, by Wall Street, and for Wall Street."

Populist Mary Elizabeth Lease, 1890

VOL. 20 NO. 503   JUNE 6 1891   PRICE 10 CENTS.

Judge

A PARTY OF PATCHES.
Grand Balloon Ascension—Cincinnati, May 20th, 1891.

In 1891, a group of 1,400 delegates from 32 states met in Cincinnati and decided to form a political party to represent working people. The People's, or Populist, party was ridiculed at the time by this cartoon on the cover of Judge *magazine. The drawing implied that the new party would be a patchwork of ideas based on a "platform of lunacy." In spite of this, the party was officially organized in 1892.*

This meant that people would be required to give a part of their earned income to the government. The party also believed that the United States government should operate and regulate the costs of transportation and communication lines.

The Democratic party controlled Southern politics, but the Populists attempted to become the challenging second party. They found great support among the black population. African Americans in the South formed their own alliance and made a connection with the white groups. Many black alliance members attended the Populist convention. The Populists realized they needed African American voters and campaigned for black civil rights.

Populism gained support not just in the South, but with farmers in the West. Populist leaders in the West were a colorful group of dissenters who hoped to lead a peaceful revolt against the powerful monopolies of the East. William Hope Harvey wanted the federal government to pay all farmers' debts and let the farmers repay the government over 20 to 30 years. Ignatius Donnelly was a Populist activist from Minnesota, who blamed big business for much of what was wrong with the country. Mary Elizabeth Lease, a farmer from Kansas who spoke widely about farmers' rights, was the Populist candidate for Kansas in the 1892 elections.

In the same year, the Populist party nominated James Weaver as their presidential candidate. The results of the 1892 elections were not what the Populists had hoped. In all, the Populists won in four states: Colorado, Idaho, Kansas, and Nevada. Overall, however, the party's candidates were defeated in both national and state elections. Even more unfortunate, the movement contributed to racial tensions in the South. Many Southern whites were unhappy when the Populists tried to unite blacks and whites. They viewed this as a threat to white economic and political power.

The Emergence of Jim Crow

Most whites in the South, and many in the North, had long believed that blacks were not equal to whites and were fearful of any social mixing of the races. Many also believed that segregation was the only means by which the races could coexist. After the end of Reconstruction, Southern society became increasingly segregated. In most areas of life, African Americans were at a disadvantage. They did not have the educational opportunities that whites enjoyed. They rarely owned land, and were often barred from holding skilled jobs that paid higher wages.

In 1828, a white entertainer had created a black character known as Jim Crow, portraying him as a foolish and ignorant person. In the 1880s, the name Jim Crow came to be used for laws and practices that separated African Americans from whites. In 1881, the state of Tennessee passed the first Jim Crow law, segregating passenger coaches on the railroads. Over the next few years, Texas, Florida, and Louisiana passed similar laws.

Eventually, the white majority in the South succeeded in removing nearly all the civil rights of blacks. African Americans were excluded from voting by various means. Southern states required that voters be able to read and write, preventing thousands of black people from voting. Because most African Americans were so poor, other laws were passed requiring voters to pay a tax. Blacks could not afford the tax and therefore they could not vote. It was a cycle that would not be broken for more than 50 years.

Plessy v. Ferguson

In 1896, a ruling by the Supreme Court gave an official stamp of approval to segregation. Homer Plessy was a Southerner who had one black great-grandparent. This meant he was one-eighth black. When he attempted to sit in a seat on a train reserved for whites, Plessy was arrested for violating the Louisiana law that segregated African American passengers from whites, and he was

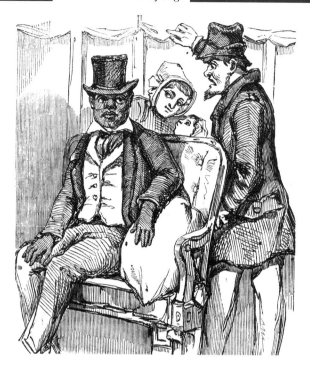

This print from the 1850s shows an early example of segregation, as a free black man is confronted by the conductor of a white railroad car. The conductor demands that the passenger move to another car reserved for African Americans.

"The slave went free; stood a brief moment in the sun; then moved back again toward slavery."

W. E. B. Du Bois, African American writer and professor of economics and history

found guilty in the state courts. Plessy then took his case to the Supreme Court, where he claimed that the state law denied his rights as a citizen under the Fourteenth Amendment. When the case, *Plessy v. Ferguson*, was heard by the Supreme Court, it established a new, "separate but equal" concept. Justice Henry Brown said that although the Fourteenth Amendment gave African Americans political equality, it did not enforce either social equality or the mixing of blacks and whites. The Supreme Court's ruling said states could legally separate races as long as "equal" accommodations were provided for both.

Nearly all the economic and social gains made by African Americans during the time of Reconstruction were significantly reversed. The Supreme Court decision allowed restaurants, stores, and other businesses to practice segregation. Jim Crow railroad cars were soon followed by Jim Crow drinking fountains, restrooms, and building entrances. In practice, the facilities were rarely equal. This was especially true in medical care and education.

Education in the South

In the North, the need for industrial skills had encouraged public education efforts throughout the 1800s. In the South, where agriculture was still the primary occupation, education did not progress as quickly. It was difficult to sustain schools among isolated rural populations, and during certain seasons, the demands of the family farm made school attendance impossible.

Schools were totally segregated. Because most politicians were white, they gave the majority of public school funds to white schools, and this left black schools with few resources. In many places, especially in the South, there were no high schools for African Americans to attend.

The New South

Even though the South lagged behind the rest of the United States in industrial development and in social progress, many Southerners saw the need to move forward. One of them was Henry Grady, the influential editor of the periodical *Atlantic Constitution*. Grady argued for the creation of a "New South" that closely resembled the North. His writings reflected the belief that the South must become more industrialized in order to prosper. This movement gained ground as industry began to take hold, aided by the expansion of the Southern railroad system.

"Cast down your bucket where you are—cast it down in making friends in every manly way of the people of all races by whom we are surrounded."

Booker T. Washington, 1895

Booker T. Washington (1856–1915)

Booker T. Washington started life as a slave, but grew up to be the most influential black man of his time. Washington was born in Virginia to a white father and black mother. He received no formal education as a young child, but he was intensely curious and taught himself to read. Washington worked in the Virginia coal mines and then attended the Hampton Institute in Virginia, a school for African Americans that taught life skills, family values, self-discipline, and social justice.

In 1881, Washington founded the Normal and Industrial Institute for Negroes in Tuskegee, Alabama, modeling it after the Hampton Institute. At first, the Tuskegee Institute focused primarily on agricultural studies, but it expanded its offerings to include business and medicine. The school quickly became known throughout the country for its excellence.

Whenever he could, Washington used his influence to increase social and educational opportunities for African Americans. In his frequent public speaking, he emphasized that education and hard work were the best paths for black advancement, rather than political reform. Others disagreed with Washington and criticized him for not fighting for black civil rights.

Richmond, Virginia, and Atlanta, Georgia, were two of the first cities that reaped the benefits of industry in the South. Industrialization soon followed the railroads and spread throughout the South. Between 1870 and the turn of the century, the South's rate of industrial growth would approach that of the North.

Public Education in America

The tradition of public education dates back to the colonial days, before the United States became an independent nation. The colony of Massachusetts passed a law as early as 1642, which said that children must be taught to read. A few years later, every town in the colony was required to have a primary school. By 1700, all the New England colonies had common schools offering free primary education.

From the earliest days of independence, education was considered important by the nation's leaders, such as Thomas Jefferson. The Land Ordinance of 1784, which was drawn up by Jefferson to divide western lands, set aside sections of public land for public primary schools. Free higher education came later, in the 1800s, as did the founding of public kindergartens.

Public education flourished in the late 1800s. In 1871, $70 million was spent on elementary and secondary education. By 1900, that figure had increased to $200 million, and 15 million American children were attending school. Between 1880 and 1900, over 5,000 new high schools were opened, but at the time only about 500,000 students attended high school.

By 1950, there were 5 million students attending high school, but only one-quarter of those who graduated went on to higher education. Educators began to look more closely at high school curricula. As a result, a new emphasis was placed on preparing students for work, not just for higher education. Schools began offering a wider range of programs, for instance home economics and carpentry. State laws also increased the number of years students were required to spend in school.

Today, the principal aims of public education are the same. Education is free, must be accessible to all, and children are required to attend school until a certain age.

Westward Expansion

While millions of Americans chose to remain in the East or in the South, millions more sought a life in a new land. In the 1800s, the railroad network opened opportunities in the West for settlers. People, and the goods they needed, could now travel from the east coast to the west coast in a week. For many, the railroads became a path to a new life.

A Mass Migration

In 1862, Congress had passed the Homestead Act. The law allowed settlers to identify an unclaimed plot of land up to 160 acres, live on it, make improvements to it, and, after five years, claim it as their own. This was known as homesteading. The law encouraged families to move west by providing sufficient land to support a family. It was unusual because it also allowed homesteading by immigrants who intended to become U.S. citizens. The Homestead Act, combined with the accessibility provided by the railroads, officially opened the West to everyone.

In the late 1800s, after the Homestead Act opened up the West, the railroads competed for the business of thousands of new travelers. This poster issued by the Chicago and Northwestern Railroad promoted the free lands and encouraged settlers to use its network to go west.

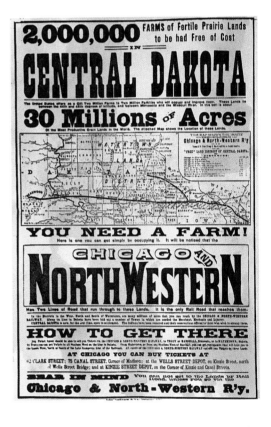

59

Unfortunately, just because the land was available, not everyone could afford to farm it. The cost of travel alone was huge, and then a family had to purchase supplies and equipment to farm the land. But those who could afford to move west became part of one of the greatest migrations in American history.

The Western Farmer

Between 1870 and 1890, a total of 9 million people moved to the Great Plains and the West, more than doubling the population in those regions. The soil was rich, and the recent advances in farming equipment made for good agricultural opportunities.

Life was not easy. Farming was still expensive, even though the land was free. In many cases, farmers needed more than the 160 acres available through the Homestead

Barbed Wire

In 1873, Joseph F. Glidden, a farmer from Illinois, went to the local county fair and saw an exhibit on wire fencing that had been invented by H. M. Rose. Rose's wire had spurs attached to it, but Glidden believed he could improve the product. He did so by holding the spurs in place using a two-braid piece of wire. It took Glidden less than a year to perfect his barbed wire. He applied for a patent and began manufacturing the wire in 1874. The product was advertised as the "greatest invention of the age," and was an immediate success, largely because it cut in half the cost of fencing property.

The demand for barbed wire was huge, and within two years, Glidden sold the patent to a manufacturing company. By 1880, the company was producing over 80 million pounds (36 million kg) of barbed wire annually.

The invention also caused problems. Cowboys, who were used to open range, or unfenced land, cut the wire to drive cattle through other people's land. Animals who were cut by the wire often suffered severe injuries. Texas cattlemen used the wire illegally to fence off public land. Still, the benefits far outweighed the problems and barbed wire soon became an invaluable part of western life.

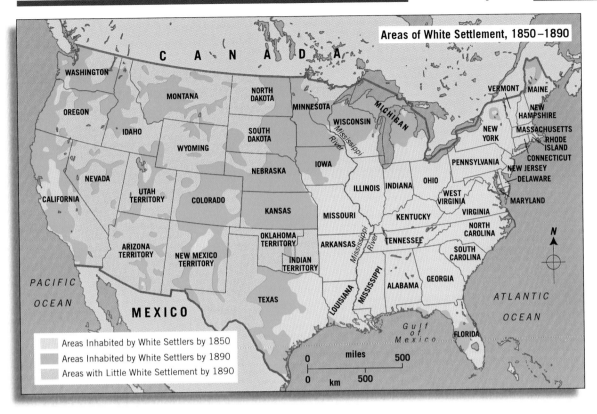

Areas of White Settlement, 1850–1890

Areas Inhabited by White Settlers by 1850
Areas Inhabited by White Settlers by 1890
Areas with Little White Settlement by 1890

Act in order to make a profit. One of the biggest expenses for farmers in the West was fencing. In 1873, however, barbed wire was invented, which was a much cheaper alternative to fencing and helped reduce the cost of farming.

The Cattlemen

Unlike the Western farmers who used the Homestead Act to gain ownership of land, ranchers and cattlemen in Texas simply took advantage of an available situation. Many had abandoned their cattle during the Civil War and the animals roamed over unfenced public lands for several years. When the ranchers returned following the war, they rounded up wild herds, branded them as their own, and rebuilt their stocks.

Like farmland in the West, the grazing land was rich. The cost of raising livestock was low and these two factors made cattle-ranching extremely profitable. Profits were helped further because ranchers continued to use public lands for grazing. They

A great westward migration took place between 1850 and 1890 as the expanded United States invited settlers. People from the South and Northeast moved onto the Great Plains, into Texas, and as far west as Oregon and California.

> "The national hero is not a prince, not a king, not a rich man—but a cowboy."
>
> *Frank Tannenbaum, historian*

> "We had buffalo for food, and their hides for clothing and for our teepees. . . . . At times we did not get enough to eat, and we were not allowed to leave the reservation to hunt. We preferred our own way of living. We were no expense to the government. All we wanted was peace and to be left alone."
>
> *Crazy Horse, Native American chief, 1877*

came to regard it as their own and assumed illegal ownership of the lands, often defending their turf with weapons.

The Southwestern ranchers had to get their cattle to Kansas or Missouri so that the animals could be sold and shipped east by rail. It only took a few men to control and "drive" many animals, but the work was long and hard, as thousands of head of cattle had to be herded over hundreds of miles.

One cattleman, Charlie Goodnight, recognized an alternative market for cattle. The growing population in the West had created a more accessible market for beef, especially among military personnel and miners. In 1866, together with Oliver Loving, Goodnight began to drive herds to Colorado instead of to the railheads in Kansas and Missouri. The new Goodnight-Loving Trail was one of four cattle trails that extended from various parts of Texas to Colorado, Kansas, Nebraska, and Missouri. During the next ten years, nearly 100 million head of cattle were driven to markets along the four trails, and huge profits were made by the cattlemen.

The era of the cattle drives was a short one. The summer of 1886 was particularly dry, leaving herds severely weakened due to a shortage of water and good grazing land. Because prices were low, many ranchers chose not to sell their stock that year. It was a tragic mistake, as the following winter was particularly harsh. Numerous blizzards hit Texas one after the other. The heavy snow and bitter cold destroyed nearly 90 percent of the Texan herds. The glory days of the ranchers were over. Although there was still a demand for beef, and they would eventually rebuild their herds, the cattlemen did not enjoy the premium prices they once had.

The Native Americans of the West

For many years, white settlement had a devastating effect on Native Americans. By the late 1800s, most Indian peoples had already been moved to reservations west of the Mississippi River. And as the century progressed, they

Massacre at Wounded Knee

In 1888, a Paiute Indian named Wovoka began to preach a message about a new world order that would restore Indians to their former place. They would once again be free to hunt buffalo and roam the Plains. According to Wovoka, all Indians were required to dance the Ghost Dance in order to return the land to Native Americans.

The Ghost Dance movement soon spread from reservation to reservation across the Plains, the Southwest, California, and the Northwest. Native Americans began to dance the special dance and to reject anything that came from white people.

Soldiers assigned to the reservations became alarmed. Reinforcements were called in and soldiers were ordered to arrest Indian leaders, including the Hunkpapa Sioux chief, Sitting Bull. In December 1890, in the course of his arrest at the Pine Ridge reservation in South Dakota, the Sioux leader was killed.

In response to this killing, another Sioux chief, Big Foot of the Miniconjou Sioux, led 350 of his people to the Pine Ridge reservation. On December 28, 1890, U.S. soldiers surrounded Big Foot's people and moved them to a camp near Wounded Knee Creek. On December 29, the army demanded the Indians' weapons. During the process, a shot was fired and soldiers immediately began firing on the camp. When the incident was over, at least 150, and perhaps as many as 300, Miniconjous were dead, and 25 U.S. soldiers had also died.

continued to lose even these remaining lands to white settlers hungry for farmland.

By 1890, there were nearly 200 Indian reservations housing 243,000 Native Americans. The conditions were generally deplorable. There was no work and no education. Indians could not vote because they were not citizens. The federal government broke its promises and treaties with the Indians time and time again. Food was promised to reservations but rarely delivered, and the supplies that did arrive were often rotten. The federal government bureau that was created to assist Native Americans instead stole their funds and supplies.

Land was taken from the Indians whenever it was wanted by whites. For example, in 1875 gold was reported in the Black Hills of Dakota Territory. The Black Hills were sacred to the Sioux tribe, and the federal government had signed a treaty in 1868 with the Sioux that gave them ownership of the land. Once gold was discovered, though, the federal government demanded that the Sioux sell the land.

There were, however, those who demanded that the government change its policies toward Native Americans. In 1885, President Cleveland returned some of the Indian lands the government had taken from them. As more and more was written about the plight of the Indians, there was a movement to pass laws that protected them. One such law, the Dawes Act, was passed in 1887. The Act was named for Henry L. Dawes, a senator from Massachusetts who believed

The Indian reservation in the Black Hills of Dakota comprised original tribal lands. The Sioux who lived there called the area Paha Sapa, the "center of the world." Gold seekers, such as this crew of miners in Deadwood, poured into Dakota Territory after 1875. The Sioux fought to keep their homeland but lost it to the white settlers.

that one answer to the Indian situation was to enable Native Americans to adopt white ways of life. The Act provided 160 acres of land for the head of an Indian family (single Native Americans were given less acreage) if he agreed to give up his tribal way of life. The Act also gave the new landowners the right to vote. Unfortunately, much of the land offered was not suitable for farming. And if it was, many Indians simply sold their acreage to whites for less than its real value. By the turn of the century, over two-thirds of the land that had been designated for Native Americans under the Dawes Act was in the hands of white settlers.

The Closing of the Frontier

In July 1893, the American Historical Society met in Chicago. One person at the conference was Frederick Jackson Turner, a young history professor from the University of Wisconsin. Turner had been studying population trends and wrote a paper on the subject called "The Significance of the Frontier in American History." In it, he declared that, because settlers had spread across the whole of the West, the American frontier no longer existed.

This photograph from 1871 shows Native Americans gathered to receive supplies of flour handed out by officers' wives at Camp Supply in the Indian Territory, in what is now Oklahoma. The territory was the largest of the Indian reservations created by the U.S. government in its attempt to confine Native Americans to certain areas. It was inhabited by many tribes who had lost their homelands elsewhere. But even this poor land was later taken away.

According to Turner, the American character was determined by a frontier attitude, a "restless, nervous energy" that drives people to explore, to expand, to move westward. He argued that, with the closing of the frontier, Americans were in danger of losing that special spirit and he suggested that people must find new frontiers to tame. The influential magazine, *Atlantic Monthly*, published the paper and suddenly Turner's views were being debated across the country. Had the frontier truly closed? Did it ever exist? Did this need to explore mean that the United States would now attempt to expand overseas?

Native American Rights

In 1924, the Snyder Act passed by Congress finally gave United States citizenship to all Native Americans born in the United States. A few years later, federal investigators concluded that the Indian policies of the previous 40 years had contributed to the miserable conditions of Native American tribes living on reservations. These conditions included poor health, little or no education, few job skills, and almost no economic opportunity. As a result, in 1934, Congress passed the Indian Reorganization Act to reduce government control of Indian affairs and give self-governing responsibilities to Native Americans.

In response to the new law, approximately 160 tribes, groups, and villages established written constitutions, built up their livestock herds, and tried to improve their economic and educational opportunities. Federal aid was given to improve schools and health facilities. The federal courts also upheld Indian treaties and agreed that property could not legally be taken from Native Americans except through fair trade. Several tribes and villages used such court decisions to reclaim land they had lost.

During the 1960s and 1970s, Native Americans gained more control over their own affairs. Through the courts, they pushed for additional rights over their land, including fishing and hunting rights, and the ownership of mineral and other resources.

Looking Beyond the Borders

Until the 1880s, Americans showed little interest in foreign affairs. As the western frontier vanished, however, the United States shifted its sights and its interest to other lands.

The Annexation of Hawaii

The Hawaiian Islands had long served as a port on the route to China. Traditionally, Hawaiians worshiped four major gods and several less important ones. Hawaiian tribes had priests who enforced religion and religious rules among their people. In 1819, the United States sent its first missionaries to the island, and 11 more missionary groups followed in the course of the nineteenth century. The American missionaries taught the Hawaiian people that their religion and their way of life was sinful. Just as they had done with Native Americans, the white Americans tried to impose their western culture, ways of dress, and Christian religion on the islanders.

The missionaries also began acquiring land in Hawaii. They established plantations and began exporting large quantities of sugar. Because the plantations needed many workers, the companies brought Chinese and Japanese immigrants in to work the fields.

In the middle and late 1800s, Hawaii was led by King Kalakaua, who was not, at first, opposed to foreign influence. However, he became concerned about the waning powers of the native population and tried to reverse the growing hold Americans had on his country. Americans in Hawaii, on the other hand, wanted the United States to annex the islands

Riches in Alaska

In the 1880s, an earlier act of expansion bore fruit for the United States. In 1867, the vast territory of Alaska had belonged to Russia. Early that year, Russia notified U.S. Secretary of State William Seward that the Czar of Russia wished to sell the Alaskan territory. Within two hours, Seward gathered his staff to meet with the Russian minister. By dawn the following morning, they had drafted a treaty for the Senate to consider. And on October 18, 1867, Alaska was transferred to the United States for the price of $7.2 million, or two cents per acre.

An 1898 issue of the Klondike News *promotes the riches to be found in Alaska.*

At the time, Alaska was viewed by Americans as a frozen wasteland with little promise for economic prosperity. Most people were shocked at the purchase, and Alaska was termed "Seward's Icebox" or "Seward's Folly."

This view was soon proved wrong. By the 1880s, salmon had become a major industry in the region. In 1878, the first salmon canning facility was built. It was just the beginning. Eventually, Alaska would become the largest salmon producer in the world.

In 1880, gold was discovered in Juneau. Six years later, another large vein of gold was found at Fortymile Creek. Then, in 1896, gold was discovered on the Klondike Creek, creating not just a gold rush, but also an awareness of the economic potential of Alaska. Barely six months after gold was discovered in the Klondike region, two ships carrying Alaskan gold docked in California. Together, they were carrying over $1.5 million in gold.

as a territory so that their companies would not be affected by Hawaiian law. In 1887, the United States did negotiate rights to establish a naval base at Pearl Harbor.

In 1891, King Kalakaua died and was replaced on the throne by Queen Liliuokalani. The queen was even more of a nationalist than the king. She was worried about the negative influence of Americans. The diets and lifestyles of Hawaiians were becoming more western. The islands were also facing problems with alcoholism and diseases introduced by white people.

In January 1893, U.S. troops were used to seize control of the islands. A provisional American government was established and Sanford B. Dole, the son of an American missionary, was chosen to lead it. At the time, however, President Cleveland rejected a proposal to annex the islands as United States territory.

The provisional government continued to rule, and five large sugar companies, which also controlled most of the banking and marketing in Hawaii, persisted in arguing for annexation. In 1898, after Republicans regained control of the White House, President McKinley asked Congress to approve annexation. Congress agreed and on July 7, 1898, Hawaii was officially annexed by the United States. A territorial government was established and Dole was selected as Hawaii's governor.

Sailors from the U.S.S. Boston form an honor guard in front of Iolani Palace during the ceremony that took place when the Hawaiian Islands were annexed by the United States in 1898.

Cuba

In the 1890s, the island of Cuba, 90 miles (145 km) from the coast of the United States, was under Spanish rule. However, Cubans were growing increasingly unhappy with their lack of independence. By 1895, violent acts by rebels against the Spanish were becoming more common. This worried those in the United States with business interests in Cuba. Americans had nearly $50 million invested in Cuba, mostly in sugarcane production.

In 1896, Spain appointed General Valeriano Weyler as the new governor of Cuba and ordered him to put down the rebels. Weyler arrested Cuban citizens believed to be aiding the rebels and sent them to camps. Cubans were outraged, as were Americans. The situation continued to deteriorate and by 1898, many feared that Americans living in Cuba were in danger.

"Remember the Maine"

In January 1898, as tension grew between Spain and the United States, President McKinley ordered the U.S.S. *Maine* from its home port in Miami to Havana Harbor in Cuba. The *Maine* was one of the United States Navy's new warships. Although the United States said it was sending the ship as a sign of faith and goodwill, it was actually there to protect American citizens and economic interests.

On the morning of February 15, 1898, an explosion tore through the ship, causing it to sink into the harbor. A total of 260 crew members died in the explosion. Americans were already angry with Spain and the sinking of the *Maine* only made the situation worse.

The wreck of the U.S.S. Maine sits in Havana Harbor in February 1898. The inquiry that took place after the explosion decided that the battleship had been destroyed by a submarine mine, but said it found no evidence "fixing the responsibility . . . upon any person or persons."

Yellow Journalism

Joseph Pulitzer was the publisher of a New York newspaper, the *World*. Pulitzer based the success of his newspaper on the belief that the *World* should have something for everyone. It ran articles on politics, finance, theater, and society. And it published the stories people loved to read most: about crime, horror, scandal, and war. William Randolph Hearst bought the New York *Evening Journal* in 1895 and began to imitate Pulitzer. He quickly drew readers from the *World* by offering even more sensational stories than Pulitzer.

Pulitzer was the first to publish a newspaper comic strip called "The Yellow Kid." The main character was printed in yellow ink, something that had not been done in a daily paper before. Eventually, Hearst stole the cartoon from the *World*. The fight over the comic strip came to symbolize the greed and lack of social conscience of the publishers. Soon, their approach to selling news became known as "yellow journalism."

When the United States entered war with Spain in 1898, the two publishers were competing fiercely for readers. Rather than reporting the news, the newspapers created it. They sensationalized almost any story just to increase readership. In fact, Pulitzer and Hearst are widely credited with whipping up the public frenzy against Spain, using the motto, "Remember the *Maine*!" Both knew that a war would keep Americans anxious for news and therefore buying newspapers.

The Yellow Kid in an advertisement for the Evening Journal.

A naval court inquiry was held, but the exact cause of the explosion was never determined. The court blamed Spain, concluding that a submarine mine had caused the explosion, but this was never proved. Democratic members of Congress used the court decision to turn people's feelings even more strongly against Spain. Word spread quickly as newspapers

> "You furnish the pictures and I'll furnish the war."
>
> *William Randolph Hearst to artist Frederic Remington, 1898*

dramatized the incident, imploring people to "Remember the *Maine!*" Americans, fed by the sensational newspaper accounts, grew more vocal about the situation. They wanted to save the Cuban people and punish the Spanish for their aggression.

The Spanish–American War

For months, President McKinley tried to calm the anger in the United States. At the same time, Spain, which was not looking forward to war with the United States, appeared ready to agree to end the warfare and grant Cubans their independence. But with public outcry growing, McKinley delivered a war message to Congress on April 11, 1898, asking for the authority to send military forces to Cuba. On April 19, Congress approved the request, agreeing at the same time to grant Cuba its independence when Spain withdrew its presence.

Spain responded immediately, declaring war against the United States on April 21. The American military fleet then blockaded the Spanish fleet in the Cuban harbor of Santiago, and American troops marched toward the town. The Spanish admiral in charge of the blocked fleet was desperate. With American land forces moving into Santiago, he decided to try to break through the harbor blockade, but his forces were defeated. In just four hours, the Spanish fleet was completely destroyed.

This photograph shows U.S. Marines in action in Cuba, during the Spanish–American War of 1898. Marines have been part of American navies since the time of the American Revolution, and became an official separate corps in 1798.

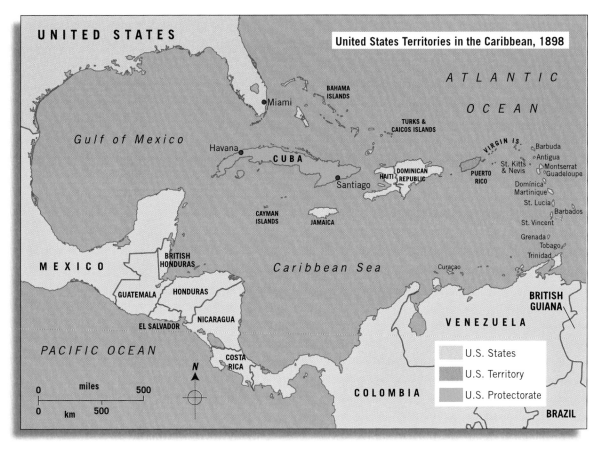

United States Territories in the Caribbean, 1898

UNITED STATES

Gulf of Mexico

Miami

BAHAMA ISLANDS

TURKS & CAICOS ISLANDS

ATLANTIC OCEAN

Havana

CUBA

Santiago

HAITI

DOMINICAN REPUBLIC

VIRGIN IS.

Barbuda
Antigua
St. Kitts & Nevis
Montserrat
Guadeloupe

PUERTO RICO

Dominica
Martinique
St. Lucia
Barbados
St. Vincent
Grenada
Tobago
Trinidad

CAYMAN ISLANDS

JAMAICA

MEXICO

BRITISH HONDURAS

GUATEMALA

HONDURAS

EL SALVADOR

NICARAGUA

Caribbean Sea

Curaçao

VENEZUELA

BRITISH GUIANA

PACIFIC OCEAN

COSTA RICA

COLOMBIA

N

miles
0   500
0   km   500

U.S. States

U.S. Territory

U.S. Protectorate

BRAZIL

Spain Surrenders to the United States

On August 12, Spain conceded defeat and agreed to withdraw from Cuba. Peace talks between the United States and Spain were held in Paris, and on December 10, 1898, Spain signed a treaty ceding Cuba to the United States. But the Spanish–American War had other results.

The Philippines, a group of islands in the Pacific, were also under Spanish control in 1898. Just days after Spain declared war, U.S. Admiral George Dewey took advantage of the situation to weaken Spanish control there. He moved into Manila Bay and destroyed an entire Spanish fleet. As a condition of the 1898 Treaty of Paris, the Spanish government agreed to sell the Philippine Islands to the United States for $20 million. Spain also gave up the island of Guam in the Pacific Ocean, and Puerto Rico, an island in the West Indies.

Soon after the U.S.S. Maine was blown up in Havana Harbor, America entered into a conflict with Spain that resulted in the acquisition of new territories in the Caribbean. Spain gave up Puerto Rico in the 1898 Treaty of Paris. At the same time, Cuba became a U.S. protectorate, which meant it was defended by the United States without actually being annexed as U.S. territory. Cuba was granted its full independence in 1902.

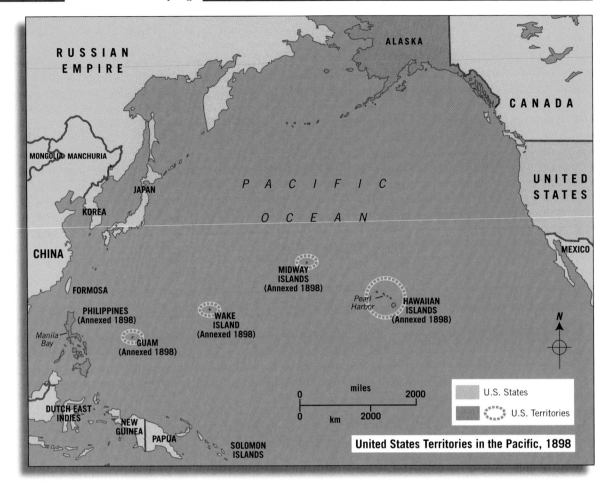

MIDWAY ISLANDS (Annexed 1898)

PHILIPPINES (Annexed 1898)

WAKE ISLAND (Annexed 1898)

GUAM (Annexed 1898)

Pearl Harbor — HAWAIIAN ISLANDS (Annexed 1898)

	miles		2000
0			
0	km	2000	

U.S. States

U.S. Territories

United States Territories in the Pacific, 1898

After the Spanish–American War, Spain ceded Guam and the Philippine Islands to the United States. This sparked a debate in Congress in 1899. Some members said that acquisition of territory in the Pacific went against American principles. Others argued that the Philippines were strategically and economically important to America.

Suddenly, America found itself with an empire. The transition was fairly smooth in Puerto Rico, and the United States established a territorial government on the island. But in the Philippines, guerrillas rebelled against American control. Over the next four years, thousands of Americans and Filipinos were killed in conflicts there. In Cuba, the rebels continued to push for full independence. Most Americans believed that had been the purpose of the war with Spain, and the U.S. government granted independence to Cuba in 1902.

The Open Door

There were other international issues. Following annexation of the Philippines, Secretary of State John Hay urged the

United States to protect American interests. The United States was becoming increasingly concerned with the aggressive attitude of the Japanese, who had been conducting small attacks on China. Britain, France, and Germany were trying to stop the Japanese and looked to the United States for help.

The United States did not intervene directly. Instead, in 1899, through a series of "Open Door" notes, Secretary Hay set forth a policy requesting that countries respect the trading rights of all other countries and not discriminate against any other power. The notes appeared to support the rights of China against Japan, but the real reason behind the Open Door notes was that the U.S. wanted to make money through trade with China. The United States did not back the policy with any definite actions, and it had few results. However, the Open Door was an important declaration of America's policy in the Far East.

Statehood for Alaska and Hawaii

World War II made Americans realize how vital Alaska and Hawaii were to United States' interests. In June 1942, Japan occupied two Alaskan islands in the Aleutian chain. It took the United States over a year to regain them. Because Alaskan sea lanes were so important to the nation, the United States Army built the Alaskan Highway in 1942, opening a transportation route between Alaska and Canada. In 1957, oil was discovered on Alaska's Kenai Peninsula. The discovery strengthened the economy, and led to the decision to allow the territory to become a state. On January 3, 1959, Alaska officially became the 49th state.

The United States entered World War II after Pearl Harbor, the American naval base in Hawaii, was attacked by the Japanese on December 7, 1941. The next day, martial law was declared on the islands and the U.S. Army governed them until October 1944. Even before the war, Hawaiians had been calling for statehood. Finally, in 1959, Congress made Hawaii the 50th state of the Union.

The New American Landscape

The rapid growth of cities and transportation routes in the late 1800s altered the way many Americans lived. Nearly every aspect of their lives, from where they lived and worked, to how they shopped and how they spent their time, was changed by the demands and opportunities of city life.

In the late 1800s and early 1900s, New York's street life was busy and colorful. The immigrant neighborhoods of the Lower East Side teemed with traffic, pedestrians, and peddlers selling their wares. By 1890, over one-third of the populations of New York City and Boston was made up of immigrants.

Urban Growth

Eastern and Midwestern cities remained the largest in the country. By 1890, New York, Chicago, and Philadelphia all had populations of over a million, and other urban areas were also seeing significant gains in population. New Orleans, Denver, and San Francisco were all growing at a frantic pace. Typically, such growth still followed industry. Birmingham,

Alabama, for example, did not even exist in 1870. Yet, once coal and iron were discovered in the area, eight businesses opened there and 26,000 people moved to the new city.

People moved to the cities from rural areas of the United States in large numbers. Most people who came to the cities in this period followed work. Birmingham attracted those who wanted to work in the iron and steel industry. The garment district of New York attracted workers, as did the financial district. In Chicago, the meatpacking plants and railroad businesses employed thousands.

Black Migration to the Cities

Even more striking was a significant migration that began in the 1870s: that of African Americans from the South to the Northern and Western cities. Black leaders believed that the migration would benefit African Americans as whites came to realize how important they were to the labor force.

Unfortunately, that did not happen. White Americans who discriminated against immigrants were even more prejudiced against blacks. And the European immigrants, who faced prejudice themselves, were no more likely to accept African Americans as equals.

Black people were not allowed to work or shop in stores used by whites. In many cases, their children were not allowed to attend white schools. Several unions, including the Shipbuilders' Union, refused to accept African Americans. When blacks formed their own unions, some of the white union members refused to work with them. Even in the North, racism still infiltrated nearly every aspect of life in the city.

Apartments and Departments

As city populations grew, the need for housing increased. One inventive New Yorker had a perfect solution. By 1870, Rutherford Stuyvesant had built the first apartment building in the city. Although many believed Stuyvesant's idea would never be successful, his building was completely rented before it even opened. It was copied in cities across the nation.

> "We live in the age of great cities. Each successive year finds a stronger and more irresistible current sweeping in toward the centers of life."
>
> *Reverend Samuel Loomis, 1887*

Frank W. Woolworth was a store employee who one day decided to reduce the prices of several items in the store. By the end of the day, everything had sold. Woolworth knew a good thing when he saw it: In the 1870s, he opened his own five and ten cent store, seen here, in Lancaster, Pennsylvania. Within six years, he had a chain of more than 20 stores.

The growing number of city dwellers also created a huge demand for goods. Marshall Field, a store owner in Chicago, recognized the people's need to be able to purchase different types of items in one store. He opened the first department store in Chicago in 1865. Field's store was followed by other department stores in other cities. Wanamaker's opened in 1876 in Philadelphia and Filene's in Boston in 1881.

Mail-Order Shopping

Before the 1870s, people would shop in stores or buy what they needed from traveling salesmen. In 1872, Montgomery Ward, a store owner in Illinois, decided to send a catalog showing his products to farmers throughout the Midwest. Customers could order and receive the goods by mail.

A few years later, Richard Sears, a railroad worker from Minnesota, began a similar mail-order business to sell watches. He teamed up with A. C. Roebuck, a watch repairman. The business was immediately successful and it quickly branched out. Soon, Sears, Roebuck was selling almost anything needed by an American family, including a kit for building

Buildings and Bridges

Just as the railroads were important to the expansion and economy of the country, steel was vital to the expansion and economy of the cities. Until the 1800s, builders had been limited to using iron, wood, and stone. With the development of steel, engineers had a material that would allow them to build higher buildings and longer, stronger bridges.

It was in the Midwest that America's first steel structure was built. In 1874, the Eads Bridge opened in St. Louis, Missouri, spanning the great Mississippi River. Meanwhile, engineer John Augustus Roebling perfected the use of steel cable suspension as a new bridge design. Towers at each end of the bridge would anchor woven cables used to keep the bridge suspended between the towers. Using this method, Roebling designed the Brooklyn Bridge to connect the New York boroughs of Manhattan and Brooklyn. The bridge is over 6,700 feet (2,000 m) long and rises 133 feet (40 m) above the East River. Construction took 14 years and cost $15 million, but the bridge was soon worth its weight in gold. From 1883, it began carrying millions of passengers each year and allowed business to spread rapidly between the two boroughs.

In 1871, a great fire destroyed nearly one-third of the city of Chicago. Several architects, including William LeBaron Jenney, moved to the city because of the architectural possibilities that arose from the disaster. Using steel beams, Jenney designed and built a ten-story building for the Home Insurance Company in Chicago. Completed in 1885, it was the world's first skyscraper. Soon after, Louis H. Sullivan designed the Wainwright Building in St. Louis. It wasn't long before skyscrapers dotted the landscape in other cities, including New York City and Buffalo, New York.

An 1880s view of the Brooklyn Bridge across New York's rooftops.

79

a complete house! In order to reassure customers who were unused to buying things they couldn't inspect, both Sears, Roebuck and Montgomery Ward offered complete satisfaction or a full refund.

The new mail-order catalogs were especially of benefit to farmers, ranchers, and others in isolated areas. They allowed rural people to buy items unavailable in their neighborhoods and to do so without leaving home. The mail-order business brought about an important and permanent change in American shopping habits.

The 1893 World's Fair

Metropolitan areas grew so fast that they often lacked any kind of planning, particularly for recreation and leisure areas. Not much thought was given to how

The cover of the Sears, Roebuck catalog for 1899. Mail-order customers soon found that catalogs offered them more choice and lower prices than local stores.

a city should be laid out. That haphazard approach changed with the Chicago World's Fair in 1893.

The exhibition and its grounds reflected the urban lifestyle. The 1876 Centennial Exhibition in Philadelphia had been designed like an amusement park, with several pavilions of exhibits celebrating new industries. The Chicago World's Fair, on the other hand, reflected a planned, city environment that embraced all the latest conveniences. It included wide-open spaces and areas for leisure activities. There were even model homes that included furniture and proposed housing budgets. There were also buildings with exhibits dedicated to the latest inventions in electricity and manufacturing. Designed by architect David Burnham, the

One in a series of watercolors published as the "Popular Portfolio of the World's Columbian Exposition," also known as the Chicago World's Fair of 1893. This view shows the Machinery Hall, one of the buildings that housed the latest inventions in America and from around the world. The open spaces and elegant architecture were admired by many and had a significant effect on future city planning.

exhibition took the theme of "City Beautiful." The fair continued to influence urban planning for several years.

The ideas on display at the fair led directly to the creation of public parks in cities. One man who shared Burnham's vision was Frederick Law Olmsted, a landscape architect. He used 800 acres of land in New York City to create Central Park, which included a zoo, a lake, roads, and riding paths. Music played from pavilions and children launched toy boats on the lake. Skaters glided across the frozen water in the winter. The urban park was a huge success, and yet another development that was soon seen in other cities.

"We cannot all live in cities, yet nearly all seem determined to do so."

Horace Greeley, journalist, 1860s

The Emergence of Leisure Time

In the years following the war, Americans found themselves with more free time. The workday had been cut and many people had at least part of Saturday off as well as Sunday. Because they had more spending money, Americans began to look for new leisure activities.

One outlet for their time and money was the circus. In 1871, Phineas Taylor Barnum opened a traveling circus that crossed the United States by train. He charged 50 cents admission and by his third year in business was admitting 20,000 people per day. Barnum then joined with another

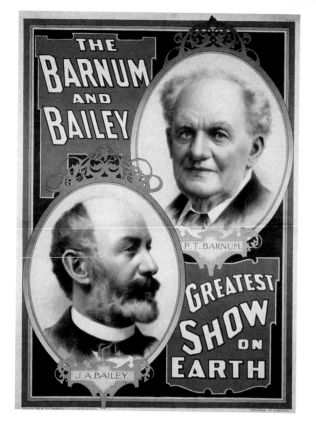

In this 1897 poster, the former rivals Barnum and Bailey advertised their joint venture as the "greatest show on earth." The public flocked to see exotic animals, unusual people, and all the dazzling tricks that made up the circus.

circus owner, James Anthony Bailey, and they formed the Barnum and Bailey's Circus in 1881.

Another traveling show was the variety show, or vaudeville. These shows contained a mixture of song, dance, and humor, and became hugely popular.

In the final years of the nineteenth century, the soda parlor also became a favorite place to spend time. The soda parlor was usually located in the local drugstore and would sell soda water combined with different types of syrups. Soda parlors also sold ice cream, which had become quite popular during the Civil War.

Sports Turn Professional

Beginning in 1869, professional sports emerged on the American scene. That year, a team known as the Cincinnati Red Stockings traveled across the country, challenging any amateur team to play them in a game of baseball. They won all 64 games they played, and became the first professional, or paid, sports team. Others quickly followed and in 1876, the National League of Professional Baseball Clubs was formed. The league established formal rules and published a schedule of games. Baseball soon became the American pastime.

In 1881, at the YMCA in Springfield, Massachusetts, a physical training instructor from Canada, James Naismith, saw a need for a new team sport that could be played indoors. Naismith created a game that suited the limitations of a confined space. He suspended goals made of peach baskets from the ceiling, divided men into two teams of seven, and the sport of basketball was born. The game was so popular that the first professional league was formed eight years later.

During the late 1880s, a trip to the seashore or lakefront became a favorite American pastime. In 1880, when these swimmers and boaters were photographed on the Massachusetts coast, bathing in public was a modest affair. Women, like the one sitting on the edge of the small boat, entered the water in heavy bathing dresses.

By the end of the century, football was still mostly a college sport, but it was growing in popularity. Stands would be filled across the country on Saturday afternoons when colleges faced one another on the football field.

As Americans found themselves with more leisure time, they began playing sports in greater numbers. Communities built tennis courts in their parks. In 1893, there were 40 golf courses in the country, but by the next year, there were 100.

Public Education

As leisure opportunities grew for those with money, others were left behind. In 1870, one in five Americans could not read or write. In many large cities, especially in the North, the public began demanding more schools. In the last quarter of the nineteenth century, thousands of high schools were founded. School attendance also skyrocketed. In 1870, fewer than 7 million children were in school. By 1900, the number of students had grown to 15 million.

Educational reform, strongly influenced by teaching methods in Europe, was also beginning to take shape. John Dewey became a leader in the reform movement. Rather

"We may divide the struggle of the human race into two chapters. First there is the fight to get leisure. And the second great fight [is] what shall we do with our leisure once we have it?"

President James A. Garfield, 1881

83

than just focusing on the "Three Rs" ("reading, 'riting, and 'rithmetic"), Dewey and others like him believed that education should build character, citizenship, and a well-rounded person. They promoted such ideas as playgrounds, kindergartens, and activities outside school hours, all of which eventually became part of American public education.

Access to Higher Education

There were also important steps taken in America's colleges and universities. Through the Morrill College Land Grant Act of 1862, the federal government provided land grants to states to support higher education in agriculture and engineering. The act gave 30,000 acres of land for each senator and representative in a state. Universities such as Purdue, Ohio State, and Virginia Polytechnic Institute and State University were formed because of the Morrill Act. States also began funding their own schools for state residents. New teaching methods were introduced and more highly-trained teachers were attracted to the profession.

Women's colleges were also established during the late 1800s. Vassar, Wellesley, and Smith all started in the ten years following the Civil War. These colleges were soon followed by Bryn Mawr, Barnard, and Radcliffe.

The Women's Movement

Even though women had campaigned for several years for equal rights with men, little progress had been made. In 1848, the feminist Susan B. Anthony had convinced New York legislators to pass the Married Women's Property Act. The Act gave married women rights that previously belonged only to their husbands: They could now own property and keep the wages they earned. However, women were not allowed to vote, and they did not enjoy equal educational opportunities or equal wages.

The feminist movement split into a number of separate groups in the years after 1860. The split weakened their political power and influence. In 1890, however, two large

"Next in importance to freedom and justice is popular education, without which neither freedom nor justice can be permanently maintained."

President-elect James A. Garfield, 1880

Susan B. Anthony (1820–1906)

Susan Brownell Anthony was born in Adams, Massachusetts. She was the second of eight children born to a school teacher. When she was seven, her family moved to New York. By the age of 15, Anthony was teaching school herself.

Anthony was a practicing Quaker who believed that alcohol should be illegal. From 1848 until 1853, she was active in the temperance movement which opposed the use of alcohol. In 1856, she joined the American Anti-Slavery Society, organizing meetings and giving frequent lectures advocating an immediate end to slavery. After the Civil War, she continued to speak out against prejudice directed at blacks.

Anthony is best known for her fight for women's rights. In 1851, she met Elizabeth Cady Stanton, another American reformer. Stanton and Anthony were convinced that, until women won the right to vote, they would not gain other rights. The two women became active in the suffrage movement. For several years, they worked to change laws that were unfair to women and in 1869, they founded the National Woman Suffrage Association.

In 1872, Anthony registered for and voted in the presidential election in Rochester, New York. She was arrested and convicted for this offense. Anthony was elected president of the National American Woman Suffrage Association in 1892 and held this position until 1900. She died in 1906, well before the Nineteenth Amendment granted women the right to vote nationally in 1920.

Susan B. Anthony (left) with Elizabeth Cady Stanton.

groups reunited as the National American Woman Suffrage Association, led by Susan B. Anthony and Elizabeth Cady Stanton, who had also been an active feminist for many years. They focused their efforts on winning the right to vote, on bettering social conditions, and on prohibiting alcohol.

Sport in America

Sports, such as baseball, tennis, and croquet, had long been played in the United States. The leisure time brought about by the Industrial Age enabled greater numbers of wealthier Americans to participate. Before the Civil War, sporting competitions were either amateur or college events. This changed in the late

A team photo of an early professional baseball team, the Brooklyn Bridegrooms, who were the American Association champions of 1889.

1800s, as baseball and basketball became professional sports. Baseball was by far the nation's most popular sport.

Football was quick to catch on in colleges. The first college football game pitted Princeton against Rutgers in 1869. The game rapidly spread from the Ivy League colleges across the rest of the country. The first professional football game took place in Pennsylvania in 1895. During the next decade, several professional teams were formed, primarily in Pennsylvania and Ohio. The first league of professional teams was the American Professional Football Association founded in 1920. Two years later, the National Football League (NFL) was formed.

The greatest boost to professional football came later, with the widespread use of radio and then television to broadcast the games. The same is true for basketball, baseball, hockey, golf, tennis, and most other sports. Today, football, basketball, baseball, and hockey are all billion-dollar industries and sports dominate television.

Conclusion

Between 1870 and 1900, the United States underwent great changes: in transportation, in industry, in the quality of life, and in population. By the end of the Spanish–American War in 1898, the pace seemed to quicken. Big companies continued to get bigger. Industry sought greater mechanization and efficiency. In 30 years, the country evolved from one that had no time or money for leisure to one that embraced it.

The western frontier no longer existed, and the economic expansion that had begun in the Northeast moved rapidly across the continent. Farming, too, had spread to the Great Plains, overtaking agricultural production in the South. Miners followed the latest discoveries of gold, silver, coal, and iron from the South and East across the continent and into Alaska.

Changes in the workplace were dramatic. Millions of people were employed in industries that in many cases hadn't even existed a hundred years earlier. Their labor supplied an increasing demand for building materials and manufactured goods.

Meanwhile, immigrants continued to arrive in large numbers. Cities grew relentlessly. Basic services collapsed under the pressure and slums became part of the city landscape. The welfare of the poor, working conditions, child labor issues, local and national government, and the power of the industrialists—all these became issues for concern. There was bound to be a backlash against the evils of big business. Part of that backlash came from the progressive movement, made up of social reformers who were to become more active and vocal as the twentieth century arrived.

Glossary

agriculture   The work of farmers, mostly growing crops and raising livestock for food.

amendment   An addition to a formal document—for example, to the United States Constitution.

annex   To take ownership of another nation or add territory to a nation.

architect   A person who designs buildings.

blockade   To cut off an enemy area, for instance by preventing ships and supplies from going into or out of ports.

bond   A certificate promising repayment to a person who has lent money.

constitution   The basic plan and principles of a government.

Democrats   The political party founded in the 1820s and in which Southerners who supported slavery were very powerful for many years.

economics   To do with the production and use of goods and services, and the system of money that is used for the flow of goods and services.

economy   The system of money that is used for the flow of goods and services.

emigrate   To leave the country of birth and go to live in another country.

exploit   To make use of something. In the case of the robber barons using the labor of the American workforce, it means using something unfairly.

export   To send something abroad to sell or trade. An export is also the thing that is sent, such as tobacco or cotton.

federal   To do with the central, or national, government of a country rather than the regional, or state, governments.

feminist   To do with equality for women, or a person who believes in equality for women.

frontier   The edge of something known or settled. In North America, the frontier for white settlers moved as they themselves moved west onto new lands.

immigrant   A person who has left the country of his or her birth and come to live in another country.

legislation   Laws, or the making of laws.

legislature   An official group of people with the power to make laws, or the branch of government that makes laws.

migration   Movement from one place to another in search of a new place to live.

missionary — A person who goes to another country (or to another part of his or her own country) to convert the people there to his or her religion, and often to help the poor or sick.

monopoly — The ownership or control of a particular product, or the supply of a particular product, by one person or group.

nationalist — A person who is very loyal to his or her nation and its culture.

ordinance — A government regulation.

patent — The exclusive right, or to obtain the exclusive right, to produce or sell an invention.

plantation — A farm where crops, such as cotton or sugarcane, are grown, and where the work is done by large teams of workers. In the past, these workers were often slaves.

policy — A plan or way of doing things that is decided on, and then used in managing situations, making decisions, or tackling problems.

Republicans — The political party founded in 1854 to oppose the expansion of slavery.

reservation — An area of land set aside for Native American tribes whose homelands had been taken or reduced by white settlement.

segregation — The policy of keeping people from different racial or ethnic groups separate. It usually means that one group has fewer rights than another.

suffrage — The right to vote.

technology — The knowledge and ability that improves ways of doing practical things. A person performing a task using any tool, from a wooden spoon to the most complicated computer, is applying technology.

telegraph — A communication system that uses electricity to send coded signals along wires.

treaty — An agreement reached between two or more groups or countries after discussion and negotiation.

tribe — A social group that shares traditions and ways of life. Native American tribes are part of larger groups called "peoples."

veto — To use authority by refusing to approve or allow something. For instance, a president can refuse to approve laws that have been passed in Congress.

Time Line

1848   Married Women's Property Act passed in New York.

1859   First oil well drilled in Pennsylvania.

1862   Homestead Act passed by Congress.
       Morrill College Land Grant Act passed by Congress.

1864   Bessemer steel process brought to United States from England.

1865   End of Civil War.
       First department store opens in Chicago, Illinois.

1866   Goodnight-Loving cattle trail established.

1867   Patrons of Husbandry (the Grange) founded.
       United States buys Alaska from Russia.

1868   Federal government signs Treaty of Fort Laramie with Sioux Indians.

1869   Noble Order of the Knights of Labor founded.
       National Woman Suffrage Association founded.

1870   First apartment building completed in New York City.

1871   Fire destroys much of Chicago, Illinois.

1872   William "Boss" Tweed convicted of embezzlement and corruption.
       First mail-order catalog produced by Montgomery Ward.

1873   First cable car introduced in San Francisco, California.
       Financial panic caused by failure of Jay Cooke and Company starts depression.
       The Gilded Age published.
       Barbed wire invented.

1874   First electric streetcar introduced in New York City.
       Eads Bridge completed in St. Louis, Missouri.

1875   Gold deposits reported in Black Hills, South Dakota.

1876   Centennial International Exhibition in Philadelphia, Pennsylvania.
       Alexander Graham Bell obtains patent for telephone.

1877   End of Reconstruction period.
       Thomas Edison invents phonograph.
       Knights of Reliance founded.

1879   Thomas Edison invents electric light bulb.

1881   Federation of Trades and Labor Unions founded.
       First Jim Crow law passed in Tennessee.

Century of Dishonor published.

1882   First Labor Day parade in New York City.
          Chinese Exclusion Act passed by Congress.

1883   United States establishes standard time zones.
          Brooklyn Bridge completed in New York City.

1884   First fountain pen produced.
          Railroad workers strike against Union Pacific Railroad.

1885   Railroad workers strike against Missouri Pacific Railroad.
          First skyscraper completed in Chicago, Illinois.

1886   Haymarket Bombing.
          American Federation of Labor founded.
          France gives Statue of Liberty to United States.

1887   Dawes Act passed by Congress.

1889   Hull House opens in Chicago, Illinois.

1890   Sherman Antitrust Act passed by Congress.
          National American Woman Suffrage Association founded.
          How the Other Half Lives published.
          Massacre at Wounded Knee.

1892   First electric power plant opens in New York City.
          Homestead Strike.
          Populist (People's) party officially organized.
          Grover Cleveland elected president.

1893   World's Fair in Chicago, Illinois.

1894   Pullman Strike.

1896   William McKinley elected president.
          Plessy v. Ferguson ruling by Supreme Court.
          Gold discovered in Klondike region of Alaska.

1898   United States annexes Hawaiian Islands.
          Spanish–American War.
          United States acquires Cuba, Philippine Islands, Guam, and Puerto Rico from Spain under Treaty of Paris.

1899   Secretary of State John Hay issues Open Door notes.

Further Reading

Arnold, Carolina. *Children of the Settlement Houses* (Picture the American Past series). Minneapolis, MN: Carolrhoda, 1998.

Collier, C. and J. L. Collier. *A Century of Immigrants, 1820-1920* (Drama of American History series). Tarrytown, NY: Marshall Cavendish, 1999.

Colman, Penny. *Strike! The Bitter Struggle of American Workers from Colonial Times to the Present.* Brookfield, CT: Millbrook, 1995.

Fleming, Alice. *P.T. Barnum: The World's Greatest Showman.* New York: Walker, 1993.

Gay, Kathlyn and Martin K. Gay. *The Spanish American War* (Voices from the Past series). Brookfield, CT: Twenty-First Century Books, 1995.

Harvey, Bonnie. *Jane Addams: Nobel Prize Winner and Founder of Hull House* (Historical American Biographies series). Springfield, NJ: Enslow, 1998.

Haskins, James. *Separate but Not Equal: The Dream and the Struggle.* New York: Scholastic, 1997.

Kent, Zachary. *Andrew Carnegie: Steel King and Friend to Librarians* (Historical American Biographies series). Springfield, NJ: Enslow, 1999.

McClerran, Alice. *Ghost Dance.* New York: Houghton Mifflin, 1995.

Twain, Mark. *The Adventures of Huckleberry Finn* (Classics series). New York: Simon & Schuster Children's, 1999.

Wheeler, Leslie. *Events that Changed American History* (Twenty Events series). Austin, TX: Raintree Steck-Vaughn, 1993.

Websites

Ellis Island – The Statue of Liberty-Ellis Island Foundation, Inc. invites you to explore Ellis Island and its fascinating immigration museum. www.ellisisland.org/

The American Experience: Suffrage History – A complete history of the American suffrage movement. www.pbs.org/onewoman/suffrage.html

A Short History of American Labor – A brief history of more than 100 years of the modern trade union movement in the United States. www.unionweb.org/history.htm

Bibliography

Axelrod, Dr. Alan and Phillips, Charles. *What Every American Should Know About American History*. Holbrook, MD: Adams Media Corp., 1992.

Brinkley, Douglas. *History of the United States*. New York: Penguin Putnam, 1998.

Davis, Kenneth C. *Don't Know Much About History*. New York: Crown, 1990.

Foner, Eric. *A Short History of Reconstruction*. New York: Harper & Row, 1990.

Garraty, John Arthur. *The New Commonwealth*. New York: Harper & Row, 1968.

_____. *1,001 Things Everyone Should Know About American History*. New York: Doubleday, 1989.

Hagner, Charles J., editor. *Prelude to the Century*. Alexandria, VA: Time-Life Books, 1999.

Morris, Jeffrey B. and Richard B. Morris, editors. *Encyclopedia of American History*, seventh edition. New York: HarperCollins, 1996.

Sandler, Martin W. *This Was America*. Boston, MA: Little, Brown, 1980.

Schlereth, Thomas J. *Victorian America*. New York: HarperCollins, 1991.

Index

Populists, 21, 53–54, **54**
Puerto Rico, 73, *73*, 74
Pulitzer, Joseph, 71
Pullman, George, 33

railroads, 12–13, **13**, 14, 15, 16, 18, 19, 20, 27, 33, 51, 62, 79, 81
  as employers, 10, 12, 31, 33
  freight costs, 17, 51, 53
  segregation on, 55, 56, **56**
  in the South, 57, 58
  in the West, 59, **59**
  see also workers
ranching, 14, 61–62
Reconstruction, 6, 55, 56
recreation, 80, 81–83, **83**, 86
Republicans, 21, 23, 53, 69
Richmond, 12, 58
Riis, Jacob, 30, 42, 47
robber barons *see* industrialists
Rockefeller, John D., 17, 18, 19, 39
Roebling, John Augustus, 79
Roebuck, A. C., 78
Roosevelt, Theodore, 47

San Francisco, 11, 76
Santiago, 72, *73*
Sears, Richard, 78
Sears, Roebuck, 78, 80, **80**
segregation, 55–56, **56**, 77
service industries, 16, 30, 31, 37
settlement houses, 47
Seward, William, 68
sharecropping, 52
Sherman Antitrust Act, 20–21, 24
shopping, 76, 78, **78**, 80, **80**
Sitting Bull, 63
slavery, 6, 85
social reform, 32, 46–48, 87
soda parlors, 82
South, the, 6, 21, 29, 50, 51, 52, 53, 54, 59, 87
  attitudes to race, 54, 55–56
  education, 56, 57
  industrial growth, 57–58
Spain, 45, 69, 70, 71, 72, 73

Spanish–American War, 71, 72, **72**, 73, *73*, 74, 87
sports, 82–83, 86, **86**
Sprague, Frank. 11–12
Standard Oil, 17, 18, 19, 20
Stanton, Elizabeth Cady, 8, 85, **85**, 86
Starr, Ellen Gates, 47
Statue of Liberty, 49, **49**
steel industry, 14, 16, 17, **17**, 18, 19, 27, 28, 36, 77, 79
St. Louis, 53, 79
streetcars, 11–12, **12**, 14
strikes, 32, 33, 34, 37
  Homestead Strike, 36–37
  Pullman Strike, 33–34, **34**
Stuyvesant, Rutherford, 77
suffrage *see* voting rights
Sullivan, Louis H., 79
Supreme Court, 21, 55, 56
sweatshops, 30, **30**, 41

Tammany Hall, 44, 45, 46
telegraph, 10, 13, 14
telephones, 8, 9, 13, 14
temperance movement, 85, 86
Tennessee, 25, 52, 55
Texas, 53, 55, 60, 61, *61*, 62
textile industry, 19, 27, 28, 31, **48**
Tilden, Samuel, 45
time zones, 13
transportation. 11–13, **11**, 14, 76, 87
Treaty of Paris, 73
Turner, Henry Jackson, 65, 66
Tuskegee Institute, 57
Twain, Mark, 24
Tweed, William, 45, **45**, 46, **46**
"Tweed Ring," 46, **46**
typewriters, 8, 31, **31**

unions *see* labor movement
United States Army, 63, 69, 75
United States Marines, **72**
United States Navy
  in Cuba, 70, 72,

  in Hawaii, **69**
United States territories, 68, 69, **69**, 73, *73*, 74, *74*

Vanderbilt, Cornelius, **18**
vaudeville, 82
Virginia, 25, 52, 57
voting rights, 55, 63, 65, 84, 85, 86

Ward, Montgomery, 78, 80
Warner, Charles Dudley, 24
Washington, Booker T., 57, **57**
Waterman, Lewis E., 11
Weaver, James, 54
West, the, 14, 21, 29, 54, 59–66
  frontier of, 65–66, 67, 87
  settlement in, 59, **59**, 60, *61*, 62–63, 64, **64**, 65
women's movement, 8, 84–86
Woolworth, Frank W., **78**
workers, 14, 16, 42, 44, 55, 77, 87
  domestic, 41
  employment conditions, 20, 26, 27, 29, 30, 31, 32, 36, 37, 43, 47, 87
  factory, 6, 16, 27, 28, 29, **29**, 30, 31, 32, 37, 39, 41, 44, 47–48
  hours of work, 27, 29, 30, 32, 33, 36, 37, 43, 47–48, 81
  injuries, 26, 27, 29, 37
  mine, 26, 27, 30, 31, 32, **33**, 57
  pay, 29, 30, 31, 32, 33, 36, 37, 55, 84
  railroad, 12, 16, 31, 33, 34, **34**, 43
  segregation of, 31, 77
  self-employed, 31
  women, 29, 30, 31, **31**, 32, 41, 47
  see also child labor
  see also labor movement
World's Fair, 80–81, **81**
Wounded Knee, 63
Wovoka, 63

yellow journalism, 71

DATE DUE

FOLLETT